Hope Endures

A BIOGRAPHY OF FAITH

JENNIFER ARRINGTON

BH

For Don McGrath

Which hope we have as an anchor of the soul, both sure and steadfast...

— HEBREWS 6:19

Foreword

The following book is a deeply personal account of LeAnn McGrath's cancer journey and Jennifer Arrington's thoughts about her experiences. We have intentionally omitted the names of any doctors to ensure that the book is not perceived as a critique of medical care. We are not medical professionals; our goal for the book was to share our experiences and their profound impact on us. Our decisions and thoughts are our own. If you are facing medical care, we urge you to follow your doctors' advice.

Prologue

W e all walk around with scars and carry hidden loads. Just yesterday, I looked at the people passing me and thought of the circle of women in my life. One had recently miscarried; another friend was awaiting brain surgery; another had watched her mother-in-law die of brain cancer... and I wondered. Those are the scars I know of. But what of the dozens of people I pass each day? What are they hiding? What do they carry? How are they coping? Do they have a support system? Do they know of God's love and immutable comfort that can carry them when all hope feels lost?

A little over a year ago, LeAnn McGrath walked into my house carrying a compact black backpack attached to a thin tube snaking from under her clothes. I can still see the smile on her face, her eyes filled with a bright anticipation. "Look at me," those eyes said. "I just drove myself here, and I'm well enough to have an adventure!"

We sat outside on my patio facing the canal, and LeAnn exclaimed over the view. I live in South Florida, in a 1970s "old Florida" house that backs up onto a canal—and the canal, connected to the Intracoastal, often delivers surprises. On our first interview day, mullet jumped as if on cue, and each time, LeAnn cheered. It was almost as if the fish knew they had an appreciative audience. Sometimes, an errant manatee would swim the canal, and I secretly prayed that day would be a manatee day, because if mullet elicited that much joy from LeAnn, what would a manatee sighting do? But there were no manatees, yet LeAnn took in the jumping fish, the warm breeze off the water, and the shady mangroves, their reflection mottled by the windy surface. Perhaps on our next interview day we would see manatees!

I'll never forget the thrill I felt watching LeAnn, talking with her, and listening to her joy. It was reminiscent of that feeling I had as a young girl when someone "important" came over to play. Right then, I realized afresh how proud I was and am to call LeAnn McGrath my friend. She walked me through my two bouts of breast cancer, yet even before cancer was ever on my own radar, we were coworkers at our childrens' school and then band moms together. I was the newbie band mom, and she took me under her wing. But it was my breast cancer that brought us close; her experience was a wealth of knowledge that helped guide my own decision-making, doubts, and daily fears.

The more she helped me, the more I realized the depth of what she had lived through—what she was still living through—and the more I understood her unique story needed to be shared. As time passed, the desire to write her story became a nudge I couldn't ignore. But I resisted; I felt it was out of my wheelhouse, or it was something someone else should do. But the nudging became insistent, so I called LeAnn, and that phone call led us to that moment on my porch wishing for manatees: our first book interview visit.

During my own breast cancer experience, I spent many hours on the phone listening and learning from LeAnn. Even now, three years post-recovery, my thoughts often turn back to LeAnn. What strength did she possess to survive her multiple encounters with cancer? I know we trust the same God, yet why did I always hang up the phone feeling she had encouraged me rather than the reverse? How had she coped, and how was she coping?

When we started this book, I'm ashamed to admit I felt noble. I was going to "help" LeAnn tell her story and be a sort of therapy for her. I thought I'd encourage her, but as time went on, I realized again that she had encouraged me. And now I look back, smile, and wonder who really needed the therapy! By listening to LeAnn's story, I have gained strength and encouragement in my own post-cancer journey. I have learned to walk my road by mirroring her attitude: taking things at face value, accepting what I cannot change, and fighting for what can be changed. Her story made me stronger. Her attitude and vulnerability encouraged me. And I want the same for others. My hope is that her story will do the same for you: encourage you, strengthen you, and allow you to find hope, no matter where you are today.

The following chapters contain LeAnn's story as she

remembers it. LeAnn and I are not doctors, nor do we attempt to approach her experiences medically. Additionally, there is no judgment regarding her past treatment plans. This is simply LeAnn's story—a story we both hope and pray will encourage you and provide insights and skills as you face your own struggles. Most of all, may the following pages fill you with enduring hope.

CHAPTER 1

A Mystery Pain

1996, 1997

Six weeks into LeAnn's second pregnancy, she started having excruciating, stabbing, abdominal pain—worse than labor. It was a doubled-over, curled-on-the-floor kind of pain, and the only things that provided a measure of relief were vomiting or diarrhea.

She and her husband, Don, had planned to have their babies close together. Baby Jon was only six months old, but he had been such an easy baby. Jon was born on October 14, 1995, after an uneventful pregnancy marked only by cravings for spaghetti with meat sauce.

Jon was, however, premature by two weeks and spent the first few days of his life intubated in the NICU due to respiratory distress syndrome. The doctors gave him surfactant to speed up lung development, and within fifteen hours, his health improved, so they were able to extubate him. Don and LeAnn brought him home three days later.

LeAnn got pregnant again quickly. Parenting baby Jon

was such fun; they wanted to do it again. Jon got on a schedule, and they would play with him, putting him on their feet to get those baby laughs. Caring for Jon was a breeze—just like how Don and LeAnn met.

LeAnn met Don two days before her twenty-fifth birthday on February 23, 1991. Don's sister, Aline, was getting married, and her maid of honor was LeAnn's close friend, Janet. Janet and Aline decided to play matchmaker, so they convinced LeAnn to meet Aline's brothers, Don and Pat—specifically Don, who was single.

Reluctantly, LeAnn attended the wedding to please Janet. She instantly took a liking to Don and soon realized his roommate had been a paramedic partner of hers years earlier. This surprising fact gave her peace of mind; it was as if, on one level, she already knew Don.

LeAnn had to leave the reception early, but Janet told Don to call LeAnn and ask her on a date, and Don complied! He called LeAnn on February 25, her twenty-fifth birthday, and they made plans to go country line dancing that Thursday in Davie, Florida. They danced for hours and ended the evening at a restaurant before Don brought LeAnn home.

The date had gone so well, they planned an outing for the following Saturday. They kicked off the day at a country concert, had lunch, watched airplanes take off, attended Don's nephew's baseball game, and ended at Southport Raw Bar in Fort Lauderdale along the 17th Street causeway.

That evening ended with their first kiss. Don then admitted he'd like to see her again, and LeAnn told him she had church the following day and a shift afterward. Straight away, Don agreed to go; he didn't mind that their next date in a few hours included church. Instead, Don said he would pick her up at nine a.m. for Sunday School and church even though he didn't attend anywhere.

After a year of attending church with her, fellowshipping with her friends, and being mentored by their pastor, Don became a believer in February 1992. In April of 1993, Don and LeAnn were married.

Now, as new parents, LeAnn worked nights part-time as a unit secretary for labor and delivery at St. Mary's Hospital while Don worked from home. This way, they could care for Jon at home and still earn sufficient income to make ends meet.

But the pain changed everything.

LeAnn felt as if someone had flipped a switch; one moment, there was no pain, and then suddenly, it was there, screaming for her attention. Don called their neighbor to watch Jon, then he rushed LeAnn to the ER.

And so began an on-and-off three-week hospital stay.

The doctors were baffled, and the pain was unlike anything LeAnn had ever experienced. Surely, if she were miscarrying, it would resemble menstrual cramps, but it did not.

Thankfully, LeAnn was already well established with Dr. R, her obstetrician who had delivered Jon, and he was available to manage her case. The doctors gave her the maximum-allowed doses of IV pain medicines, but LeAnn would count the hours until the next dose; four hours between doses felt too long.

This began a relentless cycle: The doctors would get the pain to a manageable level, discharge her, and then LeAnn would have to come right back to the ER. LeAnn and Don were desperate to find the source, but the doctors did not want to run extensive tests with LeAnn in the early stages of her pregnancy.

Then, after three weeks in and out of the hospital, the pain vanished.

Nobody knew why it began, and nobody understood why it stopped. It became a strangely horrendous blip in the day-to-day routine of their young family, and it was over.

Their lives went back to normal—or as close to normal as life could be, with Don running a business from their home, a ten-month-old crawling everywhere, and LeAnn pregnant and working night shifts at the hospital.

Mostly, though, LeAnn was overwhelmingly grateful she was pain free. Her sleep-deprived days were filled with park trips, library visits, and story time. Everything felt beautiful; the simple act of running errands and going to Costco and getting a hot dog was a gift. Ordinary life cloaked LeAnn with thankfulness, and she could focus on her babies and little family.

With her first pregnancy, Don and LeAnn hadn't learned Jon's gender before his birth because they wanted the surprise—but this time, LeAnn secretly found out. She was careful not to let Don know, but she blew it with her mom and stepmom. At Jon's first birthday party, they were in the baby's room. It was October, and she was due in three months. LeAnn accidentally made a reference to "she" and, of course, both women jumped at the blunder and were thrilled to find out. But somehow, the women all managed to keep it a secret from the men!

With the pregnancy counter sitting at thirty-five weeks and two days, LeAnn was at her desk at St. Mary's when her pain returned with a shocking sudden intensity, causing her to go into early labor. The pain switch flipped on so fast that the nurses right there in labor and delivery admitted her to the hospital.

It was January 13, 1997, but baby Emily wasn't due until February 17. In an attempt to prevent premature birth, the doctors gave LeAnn magnesium. Early in the morning on January 14, Dr. R ran a test to see if baby Emily's lungs were developed enough for her to survive outside of the womb. By 3 p.m., the results were in: Her lungs were ready.

Baby Emily was delivered by C-section at 7:26 p.m., weighing a healthy six pounds, twelve ounces and loudly letting the world know her lungs were perfectly fine.

During LeAnn's labor, Dr. R, had called in a general surgeon, Dr. H, to perform the C-section with him. The hope was that the general surgeon could discover the cause of LeAnn's excruciating pain, but he found nothing of significance. He said her abdominal area looked inflamed and the appendix "didn't look good," but beyond removing a precious baby girl, there was nothing to warrant surgical intervention.

After Emily's birth, the pain persisted. LeAnn ran a low-grade fever and felt unwell, but she had just weathered major surgery, so the doctors postponed running more tests to allow her body to heal.

Baby Emily stayed in the NICU for three days. Despite her prematurity, she was hale and hearty, so they moved her into LeAnn's room, where everyone quickly realized how well-developed her lungs were; all she did was scream for the next two days. LeAnn's milk had come in, so the newborn's dissatisfaction was not for lack of milk, and LeAnn worried those "safe" doses of pain meds may have bothered her baby. Emily ate, and Emily screamed.

On the fifth day postpartum, LeAnn and Emily were allowed to go home, and thankfully, baby Emily stopped screaming.

For the next two weeks, LeAnn lived in a fog. Fifteen-month-old Jon was a typical toddler, running around the house and getting into everything. He climbed the patio furniture, shelves, the kitchen counters, the closets, and even trees. Subsequently, Don built a play yard outside: a big wooden swing set with a slide going into a sandpit.

Jon also loved LeAnn's mixing bowls. His love for music already evident, he would drum on the bottom of mixing bowls with a butter knife. He also loved to play in water, so Don set up a kiddie pool in their backyard.

Amid all this toddler energy, LeAnn had to care for baby Emily. LeAnn was breastfeeding, not eating, losing weight, and exhausted. Finally, she visited her GI doctor, Dr. S, who ordered a CT scan.

The CT scan happened on a Thursday, and on Friday,

the surgeon, Dr. H, who was in the operating room when LeAnn delivered Emily, said she needed surgery that same night. The diagnosis: possible diverticulitis.

To this day, LeAnn is not sure if the doctors actually thought it was diverticulitis or if they were trying to sugarcoat a frightening reality. She told them, "Listen, I've been in the medical field, I know how weekends are, and I need the weekend. I need to organize my life. I have a two-week-old and a fifteen-month-old."

So, LeAnn spent the weekend arranging childcare, preparing bottles, and organizing her house. Thankfully, by the time she had children, her mom was a good grandma who could be trusted to help with the babies while LeAnn was in the hospital.

Throughout LeAnn's childhood, her mom had been addicted to pain pills. On Wednesdays, her mom's days off, she would pick LeAnn up from elementary school and drive to a different pharmacy to get her prescriptions. Each time, the prescription was under a different name.

"Why do you use a different name?" LeAnn would ask. "Don't question me," came the curt response.

They drove to pharmacies across the entire county—as far west as Davie, north to the Palm Beach County line, and south to the Dade County line. It wasn't until LeAnn was eleven that she finally understood her mom was abusing these drugs and using aliases.

At nineteen, LeAnn decided it was time to intervene. One day, LeAnn snuck one of the six or seven pill bottles from her mother's purse while her mother pumped gas.

That night, using the label from the pill bottle, she called the pharmacy and alerted them that her mom was getting drugs illegally through their pharmacy.

Still, that pharmacy filled another prescription. Frustrated, LeAnn called again and reminded them they were part of her mom's scam. "You need to tag her name," LeAnn warned. This time, the pharmacist thanked her and seemed to take her seriously.

LeAnn shared the dilemma with a family friend, Joel, who was in law enforcement. Joel listened and assured her it would all be taken care of, but she would need patience. He told her, "I know this can be difficult. You need to leave this with me and carry on with your life."

Two months later, LeAnn's mom went to a pharmacy in Hollywood during her lunch break. When she left the pharmacy, the police were waiting to arrest her and book her into jail in Fort Lauderdale.

LeAnn was at home folding laundry when Joel knocked on the door and told her her mom was in custody. Her mom was telling everyone she was still married to LeAnn's father, since he worked in law enforcement. Ironically, LeAnn's stepmom worked for the state attorney, and his office was on the sixth floor of the same building where her mom was now in jail.

Yet, instead of relief this might be the catalyst to her mom finally getting clean, LeAnn felt terrible guilt and worried incessantly. Finally, unable to rest, she called some of her closest youth group friends, and they all went to the jail to try to bail her mom out.

Once at the jail, it was as if the receptionist sitting in the window saw LeAnn and understood her life; she recognized the conflicted feelings of guilt and worry crashing through LeAnn's young mind. "Sweetie," the lady said, "your mom will be fine. She'll be let out on her own recognizance."

"But there's bad people in jail," LeAnn said, "I don't want her to be hurt."

"You don't worry about it. You just go home and go to bed."

So, LeAnn acquiesced, leaving with her friends and returning to the empty house.

After LeAnn's mom was released the following day, she laid the guilt on thick, telling LeAnn how awful the night had been. She kept repeating the warden had given her a sandwich for dinner, and she had used it for a pillow. Although her mom did not appreciate the intervention at the time, years later, she admitted LeAnn saved her life.

Still, throughout her life, LeAnn's mom would try to convince LeAnn's friends to take her to different pharmacies to try to get a prescription. But since then, the drug database has improved, and it helps prevent prescription drug abuse, making it harder to play the game.

Thankfully, too, when the babies needed her, LeAnn's mom was clean, and LeAnn and Don could trust her.

Jennifer's Take:

Medical testing upends our lives. The pendulum of

worry swings between wanting a reason and wanting no reason. With the pendulum on the "reason" side, you know you'll be able to address whatever sent you for testing, whether it's for pain like LeAnn experienced, or for another disturbing diagnosis. Your pain has a cause and should be treatable, right? But what if the reason is bad? What if it's very bad? What if it's not treatable? So, your pendulum swings back to the "no reason" side. So, now you have pain and are wishing for no apparent cause. Is that such a terrible thing? Can you learn to live with that pain?

Since my own breast cancer diagnoses and treatments, I often find myself dealing with what I call "meaningless pain." Because I've had cancer, I can't ignore pain. So, off I go for medical testing and unclear results. Cysts are the worst but also the best. They have their own swing of the pendulum. A cyst can initially look bad and lead you down the dreaded "M" road—metastasis. But most cysts are benign and just fine, which further testing clarifies.

But nothing happens quickly, and often you spend weeks wondering. All the while, your pendulum is swinging back and forth, and while you wait, your life is upended. It is a vicious cycle of ups and downs, of vacillating between hope and despair. And when I think of LeAnn's first encounter with an uncertain pain, I can't imagine how frightening it was. She was pregnant. She didn't have a reason. And then, with a tiny baby, she was suddenly sent to surgery.

CHAPTER 2

Cancer #1

1997

L eAnn nursed Emily that weekend with trepidation and anxiety. Her thoughts were all over the place: How would they do surgery on her two-week postpartum abdomen? Where would they cut her? What would they find?

She even called Dr. H and asked him how he would do surgery on her scarred stomach. "You don't need to worry about that," he replied. "The scar will be vertical in a completely different place."

Overriding everything was the relentless pain, as if her postpartum hormones had exacerbated whatever was happening.

LeAnn went into the hospital on Sunday night on Valentine's Day weekend. On Monday, the doctors did a Gastrografin enema, a scan to illuminate the colon, what LeAnn calls "a horrid procedure."

Early Tuesday morning, she went into surgery. Dr. H

did a colon resection, removing one foot of her colon and some of her small intestine.

LeAnn woke up in the elevator with Don leaning over her. "How are the kids?" she asked.

"They are fine," he said.

"Was it cancer?"

"Yes," he said.

The pathologist was present during surgery and had confirmed their worst fears. Her pain had a name: colon cancer.

Three days later, her lymph node pathology came back negative. The whole floor must have heard them scream and cry with relief. With one piece of good news, the saga was over: The tumor had been contained and completely removed.

LeAnn's encounter with cancer connected her with the best oncologist, Dr. GS. LeAnn loved Dr. GS. He was the best and acted like a bulldog with respect to the care he expected for his patients. He came to see LeAnn in the hospital and was such a kind gentleman.

LeAnn turned thirty-one on February 25, the week after surgery, and returned home to her life, free of pain, ready to recover and return to normal. There was no cancer history in her family, and, aside from this frightening event, no reason to suspect that cancer would mar any future days.

LeAnn spent the next month healing at home. Her mom stayed for two weeks after her discharge, and then her mom, stepmom, church ladies, and neighbors all tag-teamed to keep the family functioning and fed.

Those first few days at home, LeAnn felt completely overwhelmed. She had cancer, she had to begin chemo treatments, she had the responsibility of caring for two babies, and she had a home to run. How would she cope? But then she got her head about her, and she felt her mind grasp it all. No. Big. Deal.

Chemotherapy commenced when Emily was six weeks old. LeAnn had six cycles of six weeks on and two weeks off, which continued relentlessly until October. Thankfully, her bloodwork was within normal parameters every week, so she never had to miss a dose.

In the beginning, the chemo did not affect her much, but over time, chemo has a cumulative effect, and by July, she felt like a zombie. After each Friday treatment, she would begin to improve by the following Wednesday, and the fog and nausea would lift just in time for her to be lambasted again the next Friday.

One night, she attempted to attend a spaghetti dinner at church. By the time she arrived, she realized what a colossal miscalculation she had made. So, they turned around and went home. After that, she was afraid to go anywhere.

LeAnn's hair thinned, and she went on autopilot. Despite this, she took in another child to babysit for extra income. By then, Don had closed his business and started subcontracting for ten dollars an hour. They had a one-hundred-dollar-a-month food budget. The family ate rice and beans and bought whole milk for the babies. But rice and beans can be very satisfying, and they were content. Philippians 4:19 rang true: God did supply all their needs!

A couple of times, LeAnn had to take both the kids to chemo. When that happened, they would give her a separate consulting room. LeAnn came prepared with bottles and diapers and would make a pallet on the floor for the babies while she received her chemo. Her nurses would help her care for them and were incredibly loving and kind.

Chemo ended on October 13, 1997—Friday the 13th. (Who says that's a bad luck day?) The next day, they had a birthday party for Jon. He was two years old. LeAnn spent hours preparing and decorated cups with all the children's names. Her stepmom made the birthday cake. The theme was balloons, and the children all played outside. The party was a fabulous success, and she felt wonderful.

LeAnn healed and got stronger. The entire experience felt like a seven-month bump in the road. It wasn't anything to dwell on. It had happened, then it was done. It made her think of Ecclesiastes 3:1, that there is a time and season for everything.

Oddly enough, LeAnn felt sad when the chemo ended because she did not know what to do with her Fridays. Chemo had become part of her routine, and those people were her life and her lifeline. She would miss her medical team that had cared for her and encouraged her and loved her babies. She actually looked forward to checkups, because she knew she would be able to see them.

This was not something LeAnn felt she could share with people. They would find it shocking—but being critically ill takes life so far from normal that the people helping you through it become your normal. It's not that LeAnn wanted the treatment to continue; she didn't want to keep being a "cancer person." But this was her new routine, and the people who helped her had become her support network.

She was at odds with herself, but out of the necessity of parenting young children, she quickly got back into regular life, despite finding it unsettling. She did attend a cancer support group. Both times, she left feeling like they picked at her scabs; she had lived that life and didn't need to relive it through them. So, for her, the support group was not a solution.

After two months, LeAnn's energy levels returned. She took the kids to the library. They had friends over to play or were invited to friends' houses. Waterparks were a must, and there were three to choose from. The trio visited every park within a ten-mile radius of their house. Every park had its own name, courtesy of Jon's toddler vocabulary: The Big New Park, the New Park, the Old Park, and the House Park.

Life was full and beautiful, the sun shone brighter, the toddler laughter rang sweeter, and LeAnn embraced her days with joy.

Jennifer's Take:

God is sovereign.

Because the doctors refused to do in-depth testing while LeAnn was pregnant, they never knew the reason for her pain, which ultimately became a blessing. What if they had done the testing and told her she had cancer while she was only six, seven, or eight weeks pregnant? What would or could they have done?

LeAnn doesn't know, but she is thankful she never had to decide. God decided for them. Ephesians 1:11 tells us God allows everything to work for good, and even though they spent months in the dark over her pain, LeAnn is eternally grateful she never found out until later.

God had his hand on them and protected them. God used His people, so they were never confronted with the psychological impact of living with cancer while she was pregnant. And now they have Emily, who is here for a purpose and whose life has blessed them so much.

And then my mind swings from the ramifications of anguish-filled what-ifs to LeAnn's conflicting feelings after chemo and ultimately my own breast cancer. After my mastectomy, when I went out into the public, I'd find myself worried someone would notice and yet also not notice. Noticing would embarrass me, but people not understanding what I had been through felt equally frightening.

Would I act differently? Would anyone find me odd? It felt weird to face the world, knowing I had been through trauma, yet nobody knew. Sometimes, I wanted to wear a sign in case people found me strange. "Don't mind me, I just survived breast cancer," it could state.

Most times, I wanted to hide at home, but I realized hiding was counterproductive. So, as part of my daily walk, I included a forced stop at a store—any store. I would make myself walk in, buy something small, smile at the cashier, and leave. And then I'd sit in the car, nondescript package in hand, and tell myself nobody had noticed anything abnormal; I was okay. These mini trips gave me confidence, and eventually, I gained enough mental bravado to return to day-to-day life.

This is one of the ironies of long-term health problems: The world goes on without you. You exist in a separate realm.

Yes, there is joy in the completion, but also fear: You must reenter normal life, but nothing about your life has been normal.

Once you ring the oncology office bell to celebrate the end of your chemo or radiation treatments, there needs to be some sort of halfway house. By the time treatment ends, you have been through so much and are so far removed from ordinary, trying to belong will feel counterintuitive.

You'll find addressing something about your treatment will cause everyone in your group to go quiet. People who haven't been there won't know what to do with you, and you won't know what to do with them. Support groups at this juncture can help.

But in my idealistic halfway house, I see insurance companies lining up ten group exercise sessions. Imagine, instead of that weekly chemo visit, you could attend an exercise class for other bellringers. Then, at the exercise class, they provide brochures and websites of groups you can join: survivors book club, survivors coffee meetups, support groups that fit your schedule, and safe places where you can discuss what you've been through without shutting a party down.

Imagine your nurses holding a weekly coffee time where you all can chat and catch up on your lives together. I know it sounds all pie-in-the-sky and a logistical impossibility, but going from being a fighter to a survivor doesn't mean you will fit seamlessly into the same groups you were part of before.

And, to those blessed to have avoided the journey, let your friends who haven't been so fortunate talk about their own journeys. Let's normalize the ability to open up about what we endured without being viewed as a killjoy at every party. Suppose survivors could talk about their experiences, get it off their chests, and share that memory load? Maybe healing would happen faster, and the mental difficulty of assimilating into regular life would be easier.

CHAPTER 3

Cancer # 2

2000–2003

"I need you to come into the office."

It was June 2000, and Dr. R was on the phone. LeAnn had just had an endometrial biopsy five days prior. Emily and Jon were now three and four years old.

"No. If you've got something bad to tell me, just tell me," LeAnn said.

"Are you alone?"

"The kids are here."

There was a pause. LeAnn knew there was no way around what was coming.

"You have uterine cancer," he said.

"Does this mean I can have a hysterectomy?" she asked.

"That is absolutely what this means," he said.

LeAnn's monthly bleeding had gradually and subtly become irregular, a small enough anomaly that she could ignore. Chemo had ended in October 1997, and her periods had been delayed in the three years since. However, once the

23

flow began, the bleeding lasted longer and became heavier. Now, for their outings, not only would LeAnn pack her kids' snacks, water, Goldfish, pretzels, and cheese sticks, but she would also include adequate protection for herself.

Don was growing increasingly concerned, and the situation had reached a point where no rationalization could explain away her symptoms, so LeAnn had seen her doctor.

Although the bleeding was bothersome, it wasn't frightening, and with everything she had been through, she assumed her stint with chemo had put her into perimenopause. At first, Dr. R prescribed birth control, which worsened the bleeding. She called back and was told to come in when she wasn't bleeding—but by then, it was constant.

LeAnn knew she should have told the doctor long before she did. But she assumed it was a post-chemo effect. Her favorite self-assurance became: "This just threw me into perimenopause." She knew what she knew until she was proven wrong.

After the doctor called and told her she would need a hysterectomy, she was surprisingly relieved. The bleeding had consumed her life, and for that reason, despite the gravity of the surgery, she was thrilled to remove the source.

Five days after Dr. R's phone call, LeAnn had a hysterectomy; she recovered in two weeks. Life felt golden again. She could drive, felt well, and enjoyed the relief of no longer worrying about the bleeding. Even better, the pathology came back Stage 1 with zero lymph node involvement.

It was all a gift. Yes, she had now experienced two cancers, but both cancers had a resolution.

Even though she was still in her thirties, she did not opt for hormone replacement therapy (HRT), and the sudden loss of hormones was terribly difficult. She woke up from surgery with a hot flash and suffered with them for the following ten years. But, compared to undiagnosed pain, surgeries from two cancers, and chemotherapy, the hot flashes were a miserable annoyance at best. The McGrath family of four proceeded forward as if there wasn't a bump in the road.

That fall, the kids attended school at The King's Academy (TKA), a local private Christian school, and LeAnn worked as a school bus driver. The children added T-ball, gymnastics, and Upward basketball to their days; LeAnn added subbing and working in the cafeteria to her resume.

After the second cancer, LeAnn's oncologist sent her to a genetic counselor. The initial results stated there were "unidentifiable irregularities," and the genome was awry. LeAnn tested negative for something called HNPCC, or hereditary nonpolyposis colorectal cancer, which is now termed LYNCH syndrome, named after Dr. Henry T. Lynch. In 2001, only two known mutations were attributed to this syndrome; LeAnn tested negative for both.

Later, in 2015, when she was retested, there were five known mutations, and LeAnn had one, PMS-2; she had LYNCH after all. Obviously, genetic testing has improved vastly since 2001, but back then, she was considered negative. Yet God still gave her direction despite the lack of clarity from the genetic testing.

Carriers of LYNCH are at high risk for colon, uterine, stomach, liver, breast cancer, and certain skin cancers. Even though the diagnosis of LYNCH was not present in 2001, specific abnormalities made her doctor suspect she was at risk for breast cancer. Having both colon and uterine cancer by age thirty-three was abnormal; there had to be a genetic connection, even if that connection had no name yet. LeAnn was already being screened regularly for colon cancer, and the surgeons had removed her ovaries and uterus, which narrowed the field of possible cancers to stomach, pancreatic, or breast cancer. After further research, continual prayer, and the incessant nagging in her mind, she opted for a prophylactic double mastectomy.

Much has changed regarding prophylactic mastectomy in the last twenty years, but in 2002, it was considered extreme.

People were full of advice.

"You are being overly dramatic."

"That is a really aggressive move."

"This is where our trust in God has to come in; He will not give you more than you can handle."

Of all the comments, the last one hit like a truck—or more aptly, a school bus. LeAnn was working, driving a bus, had survived cancer twice, and the fear of "what's next" kept her at a breaking point. She wanted to shout to everyone she knew that she had already been given much more than she could handle. But she left it. She knew her breasts were a risk, and she knew she didn't need the approval of others to listen to the nudging God had placed inside of her.

Removing both breasts would ensure she never got breast cancer and would give her a greater chance of mothering her children into adulthood.

It took some effort to get insurance approval for the prophylactic mastectomy, but once both her doctors wrote letters stating the procedure's necessity, they got the green light. In November 2003, Dr. H performed the double mastectomy. He put expanders in, and a few months later, she had reconstruction with Dr. P.

By then, Emily and Jon were six and eight, yet having a mom who went to the hospital was "normal" for their family. The kids took it in stride with the help of Don and LeAnn's family and network of friends. LeAnn never belabored or dramatized the point, which she hoped was healthy for her children. By the time of the surgery, LeAnn had switched to homeschooling, since even with the bus driver discount and income, they could not afford the private school. Homeschooling allowed flexibility and freedom. LeAnn still drove the bus part-time for extra income, feeling every bounce of her newly implanted expanders.

LeAnn loved to gallivant with her children. They took homeschool classes at the zoo or science museum. They attended park days with other homeschool children. They enjoyed memberships to the planetarium and Lion Country Safari. And they found their people through their local Mothers of Preschoolers (MOPS) group. LeAnn loved their MOPS meetings which typically included a craft, a speaker, food, and classes with fantastic teaching for the children.

They also enrolled in a physical education program

called Saints, where they would go early and stay late. The three-hour program met weekly, allowing Jon and Emily to have outdoor fun with other children while giving LeAnn the freedom to run errands or visit with other moms.

Yet, despite this new idyllic life and the freedom to chart their own days, the responsibility of educating her own children scared LeAnn. She was constantly afraid there would be holes in their curriculum. She also found it difficult to stay home, cover the basics, and stick to a schedule. The desire to go and do was too strong.

The worry of falling short at educating her children or being sidelined by another cancer diagnosis plagued her, but then LeAnn would remind herself she had eliminated two of the possible "big five" cancer risks. She could no longer develop breast or uterine cancer, and she was regularly monitored for the other three.

So, she lived her homeschool mom's life to its fullest, relishing the days spent with her kids, immersed in their lives, investing in their childhood, and making memories every step of the way.

Jennifer's Take:

When I reflect on our own homeschool years, I smile at the realization that we started homeschooling by accident. My eldest was ready to read, so I bought the Abeka phonics curriculum, and she learned to read before she was ready for kindergarten. Then we didn't know what to do with her! It was a good problem, though. My second child was too active for a traditional preschool program, and I didn't want her to earn a label I suspected she'd grow out of, so we just kept homeschooling.

It was a year-by-year decision, but it was a time I will cherish as some of my sweetest parenting memories: read-alouds on the porch swing, spelling words in a tree fort, writing simple problems on the glass sliding door with dry erase marker, keeping my youngest learning while constantly moving.

As a teacher, LeAnn's fear of "holes" in learning resonated with me, and I exhausted myself making sure all our bases were covered. I had also heard the phrase, as I am sure you have, "that God doesn't give us more than we can handle."

Like LeAnn, that phrase has always stopped me short; I'm not sure why Christians say it to each other. The phrase is not biblical and runs counter to the story of Job, of Joseph, of David being chased by Saul, of Jeremiah the prophet being thrown in a pit, and of the martyrs in Hebrews 11. And those are only a few examples. The fact is, God does allow more than we can handle—then we lean on Him, because no trial is too big for Him.

Sometimes I think about LeAnn's decision to have a prophylactic mastectomy before it was more commonly accepted. I got a lot of questioning for having a double mastectomy with my second breast cancer. I would answer the first question, and then sometimes the second, and then I would say something vague or change the topic. People do mean well, and we often say unhelpful things to each other, but questioning others' medical decisions is counterproductive. How can one conversation begin to replicate the thought, research, and doctor's visits that have contributed to someone's decision-making process? It can't.

I love Genesis 24:27, which states, "I being in the way, the Lord led me." We don't have to be able to predict our next steps, we just need to trust if we are "in the way" and follow God's leading, He will continue to guide us whether with medical decisions or how best to school our children.

When I consider the divine guidance that led LeAnn to a prophylactic mastectomy fifteen years before she learned she did indeed have LYNCH, my faith is strengthened. One can only guess what would have happened if she had listened to well-meaning people over the still, small voice of God. God led her, He guided her thoughts, and I fully believe LeAnn can sit on my patio and watch for manatees today because she listened to His voice!

CHAPTER 4

Cancer # 3

2006–2007

The homeschool years continued with all the ups and downs that create a chaotically enjoyable time. LeAnn was healthy the whole time, and "normal" had come to stay.

One December day in 2005, in the middle of all their busyness, The King's Academy called: Would LeAnn be willing to work in the cafeteria? The job included two free tuitions.

LeAnn always wondered where that offer came from. Everything was going well, and they had successfully home-schooled for two and a half years, so why did God redirect them again? But they took this offer as guidance from God, and LeAnn accepted the position.

The children entered school in the middle of their third- and fourth-grade years, returning to a new type of busyness. Not only did LeAnn work the cafeteria during school hours, but she also worked as a bus driver substitute for the entire spring semester of that school year.

Day-to-day life had been turned on its head; the locked-in structure of traditional schooling was a shock to their systems (both academically and socially) after home-schooling.

Once they adjusted to a more regimented life, LeAnn realized it was just what their family needed. Genesis 24:27 played out in their lives: They had been "in the way," and God had "led them." LeAnn felt relief that she no longer had to worry about holes in her children's curriculum, and the children found their niches.

Jon's teacher, in particular, brought to light his bent toward music and math. And, although they missed their homeschooling days, The King's Academy was absolutely the right choice for that time in their lives. By the end of the semester, the routine of their new days had become second nature.

Summer 2006 came, and they welcomed it with gusto. They had survived the semester of adjustment, which made this summer even sweeter. They played and divided their time between random beaches, the lagoon at DuBois Park, and nearby water parks. It was a complete time of decompression where LeAnn could enjoy her children and their time in the sun (which she has always craved) without a schedule.

Then the fall semester began with nine-year-old Emily in fourth grade and eleven-year-old Jon in fifth, and the family plowed headlong into the routine of uniforms, teachers, homework, and extracurriculars. LeAnn was well entrenched in the cafeteria and continued to drive the bus as a substitute.

In November, LeAnn went in for her regular CAT scan of the abdomen and pelvis. Her oncologist called three days before Thanksgiving; the lymph nodes in the right side of LeAnn's groin were enlarged and would need a biopsy.

This came as a complete shock. Their lives were on track, everyone was busy and productive, and there had been no warning—no telltale signs of pain, no nudge to pay attention—just the necessity to attend LeAnn's routine screening.

The doctors promised she would only feel pressure during the biopsy, but LeAnn begged to be put under anesthetic for the procedure. The medical field can often feel cold, and this was one of those instances where they insisted going under would be unnecessary since she would "only feel pressure." But on top of the extreme pain LeAnn felt during the biopsy, a pathologist conducted an on-site frozen section and confirmed the presence of malignant cells. That day, they left knowing LeAnn had cancer again—and because the cancer was in the lymph nodes, they were unsure whether the colon or uterine cancer had spread.

By the beginning of December, the pathology came back with the dreaded M-word: metastasis. Uterine metastasis, to be specific—Stage 4. LeAnn's doctors referred her to a gynecological oncologist, Dr. G.

Right before she met with the oncologist, LeAnn walked into the cafeteria at TKA. She spotted her friend Tracy, and LeAnn broke down. With their children only nine and eleven, her earnest prayer was that she would live long enough to put her children through TKA and see them graduate. The fear of leaving them before they graduated was unconscionable. The thought that she might not be there for those vital formative years, working the job that kept them enrolled in a school where they thrived, was horrifying and heartbreaking.

Tracy comforted her and soon, all the TKA bus ladies had surrounded her. They prayed for her healing, and they prayed LeAnn would be able to realize her dream: to see her children walk across the stage as graduates of The King's Academy.

LeAnn went into surgery on December 15, 2006, where the surgeon unsuccessfully tried to remove the lymph nodes —but the procedure failed because they were too obscured by blood vessels. Instead, Dr. G placed titanium clips to target the area for radiation.

After surgery, for the first time in any of her cancers, LeAnn went through a two-week period where she thought the uterine metastasis would kill her. She feared she would never see her children grow up. Hope felt impossible. But then her doctor called Memorial Sloan Kettering in New York, and those doctors referred her to an updated treatment plan. At that point, the veil of doom lifted, and the feeling of imminent death went away. It was encouraging to finally have a promising treatment plan.

LeAnn needed time to heal from the surgery, and because the radiation wouldn't commence until the New

Year, the family went on a trip to Washington, DC, immediately after Christmas.

That trip became a highlight of those years, a wonderful time of togetherness for the family. They couldn't afford for their children to attend the school DC trips, so they made their own. They visited Pennsylvania to connect with some friends and even go skiing. For Florida people, skiing can be the ultimate vacation since it is diametrically opposite to anything the Sunshine State offers! LeAnn sat on the sidelines and watched as her children and Don took to this sport.

In DC, their favorite spots became the Air and Space Museum and the Mall. They relished the bracing weather and hit all the highlights: the Washington Monument, the White House, and the Lincoln Memorial. Every day felt like a gift for living in the moment and not focusing on the recent diagnosis nor what was to come—for simply enjoying time as a family.

After returning from vacation, the kids went back to school, and LeAnn began radiation in January 2007. The first two weeks went well, and then the cumulative effect kicked in. Her pain was excruciating. LeAnn would curse from the pain; the radiologist targeted her entire pelvic region. She began itching, and the itching became an awful, gut-wrenching pain that tore through her body relentlessly like a flaming torch, the most intense agony she had ever experienced.

"I would not recommend it to my worst enemy," she said.

LeAnn's doctors ran chemotherapy in combination with radiation, the brand-new procedure in the cancer world. The rationale was that chemotherapy would weaken any cancer cells making them more porous to the radiation.

By week four, LeAnn was on morphine around the clock. Radiation was administered every weekday, and chemo was given once a week. Now it felt like the treatment would kill her.

And this was "mets," or metastatic cancer: The target is broad, and the treatment brutal. Healthy tissue is sacrificed to kill the invasive tissue. Due to the morphine and the intense pain, LeAnn remembers very little of those months. Yet she does remember how people rallied with help, coming out of the woodwork to assist with finances, food, and caring for their children. She knew then that God had placed her back at TKA, knowing the community would rally around her, Don, and their children. The children were established, and Mr. Loveland, the TKA president at the time, worked with her, telling her, "You come back when you are well."

God placed her at TKA for that time—even as her cancer grew. So why not just remove the cancer? Scripture says, "All things work together for good" (Romans 8:28a). So, instead of focusing on why the cancer returned, LeAnn focused on how God had placed her in a situation where her family would be able to survive the battle,

Chemo and radiation lasted through March 2007, and LeAnn returned to work for the month of May.

LeAnn's love language is service to others. When she

graduated from high school in 1984, she was working at Publix. She then trained as a dispatcher and realized taking phone calls was not for her. So, in 1985, she attended Emergency Medical Technician (EMT) school and began EMT training in July 1986. She was only twenty years old.

After being an EMT for three years, she went to paramedic school in 1989 and was a paramedic until 1996. When Jon was born, she realized she wasn't the same person and could not handle that type of sadness and stress with a baby at home. After praying, seeking counsel, and pondering all the ramifications, she and Don eventually agreed she would be a stay-at-home mom.

Eleven years later, being around the students and coworkers at TKA fulfilled LeAnn's desire to serve others. She was back around her people, collecting trays and interacting with students, and even though she would frequently have to find a stool to sit and catch her breath, she was working again! Everything about the job energized her, whether treating the staff well on their short lunch breaks, being a cashier, serving on the line, finding a shy student the warmest, newest piece of pizza; she relished every aspect of the job and loved being surrounded by people once more.

LeAnn and her family completed the school year and welcomed summertime. Although LeAnn did not have the energy of the prior summer, she was well versed in the "fake it till you make it" mindset. Fatigue and all the residual effects persisted, but LeAnn embraced the summertime with her kids and everything that meant for their family.

That summer, they managed a trip to North Carolina's

Outer Banks. So much had happened since their DC trip, but there they were, only six months later, enjoying family time once more.

After they checked into the Airbnb, they went to the beach but found the June water too cold for their Florida blood. It seemed absurd to be cold in the ocean in June, so they focused on the Wright Brothers Museum before eventually returning to the beach to soak up the sun.

One of their favorite activities were the sand dunes at Jockey's Ridge State Park. Some of the dunes are as tall as one hundred feet, and Jon and Emily would look like little pin dots while they ran up the dunes. When they raced down, they would fall and roll. The family grilled outside almost every night—hamburgers and hotdogs and chicken. There was a big pool on the property and a clubhouse with activities. They enjoyed line dancing, made tie-dyed T-shirts, and attended a movie night at the pool. It was fantastic!

On their one rainy day, they spent it in the condo together, watching movies and playing games. Not one moment was wasted on worrying about where they were in LeAnn's cancer journey; instead, they soaked up every moment of togetherness.

When they returned to school in the fall of 2007, the kids were now in fifth and sixth grade. Emily had one of the best teachers, Mrs. S., who had been through cancer herself and was a loving advocate for Emily every day at school. Emily thrived that year.

LeAnn returned to the cafeteria, but for her, the school year quickly went downhill. By September, the radiation damage reared its ugly head in the form of Small Intestine Bowel Obstructions (SIBO), and LeAnn had to go to the hospital each time it occurred.

LeAnn suffered from SIBO multiple times. The doctors would admit her and give her a nasogastric (NG) tube that ran from her nose into her stomach to suction out whatever had gotten trapped. The NG tube would typically be placed for two or three days while she stayed on a liquid diet. Many times, though, the tube would remain for as long as five days.

Radiation didn't stop when the treatment stopped. Instead, it continued its insidious yet necessary work, destroying both good and bad tissue. Because of LeAnn's prior surgeries, she had scar tissue causing adhesions, and the doctors believed the SIBO was probably the result of the adhesions.

Dr. H eventually did a surgery called "lysis of adhesions," where he scraped away the scar tissue that was causing obstruction and surgically removed a portion of her damaged small intestine.

During this time, the bulk of the parenting responsibility fell on Don. He was their Super Dad, and despite everything, the family persisted. They did not dwell on things or overexplain.

After the SIBO episodes, LeAnn's condition stabilized, and the rest of the school year went on without difficulty. "Normal" had finally returned. The family enjoyed all the Florida winter festivities and later spring break, including a camping trip to Key Largo, the largest island in the chain of islands called the Florida Keys.

The Key Largo camping trip had been part of LeAnn's life since she was in her church's singles' group, and she had probably attended for nearly twenty years, beginning in the mid-1980s. It was a biyearly event, and that spring break, the family returned; their three-room tent was the envy of all their church friends.

The Keys trip was always the epitome of relaxation. There was no timeline, no schedule, and the bay glistened right in front of their tent. The children could swim, snorkel, play, kayak, sail, and have the freedom to be outdoors surrounded by clear, blue water and endless options. LeAnn would sit with the other moms and enjoy the camaraderie of companionship surrounded by beauty.

The McGraths came ahead of the other campers and set up first. Then, as other members of their group would arrive, they helped them set up. Everyone had small children, so everyone needed help. Their campsite was where everyone came to get what they had forgotten: a leaf blower, flashlights, a fire starter, extra pots and pans, clothes detergent, and even three kinds of bug spray.

Once everyone was ready, they would all go to a restaurant together, ready to celebrate the start of yet another Florida Keys weekend. It was a symbol of beginnings, and for the McGraths, it was a chance to celebrate another reprieve from cancer and to immerse themselves in "normal" with a group of friends who had prayed them through another difficult road.

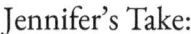

Jennifer's Take:

I cringed when LeAnn recounted the story of her lymph node biopsy. Until my first breast biopsy, I was a bit naïve concerning how invasive such things could be. I have had multiple skin biopsies over the last twenty-five years, and for some reason my brain catalogued a breast biopsy as the same thing. But it wasn't the same thing—not even close.

I had five breast biopsies, and four of them were exceedingly painful. In fact, a big factor in me agreeing to my double mastectomy after my second breast cancer diagnosis was the thought that, without breasts, I would never have another breast biopsy!

I'm all about being prepared before a procedure or surgery. So, before my first breast biopsy, I researched and even watched YouTube videos of what to expect. To be honest, it didn't seem like a very big deal. So, I went in, still picturing an event similar to a skin biopsy, and left completely wrecked.

Now, I'm fully aware many people experience the YouTube version of breast biopsies; my fifth one was exactly as depicted and actually no big deal. But I wish I had known it could be so much more difficult—not because my goal is to scare people, but to prepare people.

Case in point: A friend of mine had a breast biopsy and called me after the event to tell me how embarrassed she was about her reaction to it. She had also gone in thinking "no big deal," and was thus unprepared. Other women were present, and theirs had been routine. But hers, like mine, was not. Sometimes the doctor can't grab enough tissue; sometimes the lump is deep and hard to access; sometimes the tissue is very dense and acts impenetrable. I talked with my friend and promised her she didn't cry and pass out because she was weaker than the other women, but because some biopsies can be awful. Her shame over her body's reaction to the trauma was completely unwarranted. She wasn't weak; she simply didn't realize how difficult it might be.

And that's why I warn people to go in prepared, to have someone drive them, and to purchase those gel eye patches that you can freeze and slip into your bra afterwards. I warn them it may take a while to stop bleeding, which will lengthen their time at the office. And, if their experience is "normal," they can leave thankful. But if their experience is difficult, they can know it wasn't because they weren't brave enough or "good enough," but because sometimes biopsies are difficult and painful.

Now, enough of biopsies! Let's flip the script and talk about something more pleasant: those McGrath vacations.

Did anyone else think how magnificent it was that the McGraths took two glorious vacations in the middle of the trauma of metastasis treatment? What a beautiful lesson this was to me. Here her family was in the middle of their darkest trial to date, and they went on vacation—twice. They immersed themselves in those vacations; they lived in the moments; they made memories together; and LeAnn still gets a twinkle in her eye as she recounts them.

Wow.

I am now determined not to allow looming clouds to ruin a perfect day. Today, where I am, is a gift. That pendulum of testing and waiting happens often now in our family. It seems we can't stay in the clear for more than a few months at a time. But we do have a choice. We can enjoy the day in the waiting and immerse ourselves in the gifts around us, because that's what Jesus wants us to do! In His sermon on the mount, Jesus tells us in Matthew 6:34 to "Take therefore no thought for the morrow: for the morrow shall take thought for the things of itself." So, when I catch myself ruminating or extrapolating into frightening territories, I quote this verse and encourage myself: Live today because today is promised, and don't borrow worry from tomorrow!

CHAPTER 5

Years of Reprieve

2007–2015

A fter battling three cancers on and off over a decade, life seemed to stabilize. Even though ten-year-old Emily, eleven-year-old Jon, and Don had lived alongside LeAnn throughout these dark and difficult ordeals, the family righted itself and thrived.

By seventh grade, Jon was part of a concert band and had chosen percussion. By ninth grade, he added the bass guitar to his repertoire. With both bass guitar and drums as the background of any song, Jon had found his passion. Emily, in the meantime, was learning the flute.

The TKA bands provided both Emily and Jon a strong connection to their school. They had finally found their place. The band provided a school family, a purpose, and a healthy environment. It transformed Jon, giving him a meaning and the opportunity to be in leadership. This was the community Jon and Emily were part of, and Emily, four years older than Jennifer's daughter, became her band mentor. It was an incredible way to help her feel a sense of belonging. They were secret pals together, and they even shared the same birthday.

Those years were blissful; the McGraths embraced life, and the band remained front and center. They attended marching band competitions where Don and LeAnn moonlighted as full-time band parents and helped transport equipment to and from competitions, cheering for their kids. Don was the roadie, and LeAnn helped prepare the stands for the home football games—organizing snacks, preparing the drinks, and filling the coolers.

Jon and Emily were also in the orchestra pit, playing in various musicals including *Cinderella, Beauty and the Beast, Les Miserables, Hunchback of Notre Dame, Phantom of the Opera, Aida,* and *Titanic.*

Jon and Emily had a series of inside jokes on the music from the performances. The song "Topsy Turvy" was weird to play, so they called it "Toxic Turkey." Then there were other funky names they created, the original titles long forgotten, names like "Chernobyl Warbler," "Funky Finch," and "Thunder Chicken."

LeAnn sat in the front row for *Les Miserables*, where she was eye to eye with one of the students singing "Bring Him Home." LeAnn started crying as the poignant music played and the profound words washed over her. The young man, singing his heart out, saw her tears and seemed surprised at her reaction, but all LeAnn could wonder was whether those words would be true for her. Would God hear her prayers? Would He provide peace and rest?

When Jon was in eleventh grade, Don helped him build a slap organ out of PVC pipe and played with flip flops. They had seen it on YouTube and decided to make their own. Don bought a stash of Old Navy $1.99 flip flops, so if one broke, there would be an immediate replacement. His inaugural performance is available on YouTube under "PVC Pipe Instrument – Forte! 2013." Enjoy!

Jon graduated in 2014, and LeAnn realized the first part of her overarching goals: to live long enough to see her children graduate from The King's Academy. Jon started at Palm Beach State College, studying music and playing gigs on the side. Now only needing one TKA tuition break, LeAnn dropped to part-time work at TKA and earned her CNA license during Emily's senior year. Emily graduated in May 2015.

When Emily walked across the graduation stage in May 2015, all LeAnn could think was how God had directly answered her prayers. Emily looked beautiful, a true testament to everything LeAnn had prayed for—to watch both her children graduate from The King's Academy. LeAnn had realized her goal. She thought back to 2006 and pictured herself warped with fear, sobbing in front of the cafeteria, surrounded by her coworkers, just begging the Lord to let her live long enough for this moment. He had seen and answered that prayer.

With her children graduated and pursuing degrees—Jon in music and Emily in psychology—LeAnn returned to the hospital for genetic testing. She wanted definitive results so her children could make informed decisions. LeAnn received her results in June 2015: She was positive for one of the five known LYNCH mutations. (As mentioned earlier, LeAnn's testing in 2001 was negative, but back then, there were only two known mutations.)

The family met with a genetic counselor, Robin, who spoke with Jon and Emily, as they were now old enough to provide permission for their own testing. When the results came back, Robin called Jon first and told him he was negative, but she was about to call Emily, and Emily would need his support.

After talking with Emily, Robin called LeAnn. Robin addressed LeAnn as "Mom" and this gave LeAnn a measure of support. She couldn't give Emily's results to LeAnn, but she told LeAnn to call her daughter. For LeAnn, that day stands out as one of the hardest. It is one thing to live with bad news for yourself, but it's completely heartbreaking when the bad news is for your child.

They all talked, and they cried, and Jon reiterated he wished it could have been him. But LeAnn told him that although she didn't want it to be either of them, she knew Emily would be proactive and stick to the testing schedule.

The maintenance testing means regular breast exams, a yearly colonoscopy, an upper endoscopy, and mammogram every other year, and an endoscopic ultrasound (EUS) every five years, which allows the doctors to view the pancreas.

It's been nine years now, and Emily has always been clear. And this is the benefit of genetic testing: She can be vigilant and have peace of mind. The possibility for cancer gives the impetus to get regular screening. If the doctors find something, it will be caught early and will be treatable. But at the same time, Emily can live without a cloud of fear. Her vigilance gives her the freedom to live!

According to the CDC, LYNCH Syndrome is the most common cause of hereditary colon cancer. People with LYNCH Syndrome have inherited mutations in the genes that fix mistakes after DNA is copied. If these genes cannot correct errors, the risk of cancer increases. But just because someone has the mutations does not mean they will necessarily get cancer. So, the presence of the genetic condition is more of a case of "knowledge is power" and can help patients catch any possible cancers early.

Jennifer's Take:

As I reread this section, I am reminded how God cycles people through our lives. Sometimes people cycle through for a short time, and sometimes repeatedly. LeAnn went from being my coworker to a fellow band mom to a partner in crime trading cancer stories, and now she is a dear friend whom I feel deeply honored to write about. As God has allowed our lives to intersect at increasingly deepening levels, I am both awed and grateful. This chapter reminds me of all those levels.

It was 2010 when I met LeAnn for the first time. I had just returned to TKA after taking a break from teaching to homeschool my own children. As I searched for gluten-free food options in the cafeteria—feeling stressed, new, and frustrated with myself for forgetting my lunch at home—I ran into LeAnn. I don't remember what LeAnn said to me, but I remember she made me laugh. From then on, if I had to go to the cafeteria, I would go to her cash register just to hear one of her one-liners. There was always a reason to smile after an encounter with LeAnn.

Then, a few years later, my eighth-grade daughter joined band. My husband and I helped as new band parents, and I got to know band mom LeAnn better. I'll never forget sitting at breakfast one Sunday morning after the state band competitions in Tampa, explaining to LeAnn I wasn't eating because I had a colonoscopy the following day. In response, LeAnn told me how best to get through it, and that's when I first learned of her cancer story. LeAnn never wore her cancer like a badge of nobility to be nursed or paraded in front of others, but when someone needed advice or a sympathetic ear, she was ready—a soldier equipped to help and heal.

Part of LeAnn's equipping is her encouragement regarding genetic testing. Once I knew I had cancer again, I talked regularly with LeAnn, and our friendship deepened. She not only gave me advice as I looked at the myriad treatment choices I had, but she also encouraged me regarding genetic testing.

Case in point: I found my second breast cancer so quickly it was only 0.7mm with zero lymph node involvement. After the first cancer, I had genetic testing, and my diligence was dialed up; I didn't skip mammograms as I had before the first cancer. Even though my genetic testing came back "VUS" or variants of uncertain significance, I was now hyperaware of my symptoms. The doctors applauded me for catching my second one so quickly, but I was only doing what I had been taught: getting genetic testing, watching for changes in the skin, checking for lumps, and scheduling my follow-up mammograms.

This latest cycle includes our closeness, which has grown while writing LeAnn's story. One of the hardest days for me involved listening to LeAnn explain her thoughts and feelings regarding the LYNCH testing. All I could think was if it was hard for me, how heartbreaking it must have been for LeAnn. But, as they had after getting knocked to the ground by other bad news, the family righted itself. Knowledge is power, and regular testing can prevent anything catastrophic from happening, because genetic testing provides valuable information and directs care.

I know some may wonder at the wisdom of genetic testing, but I believe it allows us to make sound, informed decisions based on what we know. We don't hide our heads in a hole and worry. We push through the circumstances we are handed, put safeguards in place, and then go enjoy the day God has gifted us.

As I consider how God places people in our lives for a purpose, I can't help but thank Him for the gift of LeAnn's friendship—for all she has taught and encouraged me, and that, because of her, I stay vigilant with my own tests and scans and procedures. It makes me think of the words of Proverbs 27:17 and I am eternally grateful: "Iron sharpeneth iron; so a man sharpeneth the countenance of his friend."

CHAPTER 6

Cancer # 4

2015

I n August 2015, almost nineteen years since LeAnn's first colon cancer, she went in for her yearly scan. At this point, the scans seemed unnecessary, and LeAnn was over them. To that end, right before Dr. S put her under anesthesia, LeAnn told him this would be her last colonoscopy. Every single one had been clear, and it felt unnecessary to continue.

After LeAnn woke, she got dressed and went to the private waiting area where Dr. S met his patients to go over the scan. When LeAnn walked in, Don was waiting for her, which was not the norm. As soon as LeAnn sat down, Dr. S came in.

There was a mass on her right side. LeAnn needed surgery.

The irony.

And just like that, their lives were upended—again.

Yet life went on. There were already plans in place to

take Emily to UNF for her freshman semester. So, LeAnn determined she and Don would rent an Airbnb an hour away in the town of Palm Coast. This would be their first vacation as "empty nesters," but the real reason was that LeAnn wanted to be within "spitting distance" of Emily. That way, anything Emily needed—even, as LeAnn put it, a USB cord or some snacks—they would be close enough to help.

By now, the pathology was back from her colonoscopy. LeAnn had colon cancer again.

The nine-year cancer hiatus was over, and the irony of the timing, so close to Emily's graduation, did not escape LeAnn. But they rolled with it, as they had rolled with the other three diagnoses, and moved forward with the planned college move-in and mini vacation. LeAnn's goal was for everything to feel as normal as possible so Emily could focus on her first year and not worry about her mom.

LeAnn took this diagnosis harder than the others. She felt gutted, in disbelief, possibly because it had been so long since a diagnosis. But, once she adjusted to the reality, she focused on the task at hand: They would do as they had done before. Don's phrase was "Do the thing." They would face it together and "do the thing," one step at a time.

To add to the anxiety, though, Hurricane Fred was brewing in the Atlantic, and between the possibility of a storm and the impending surgery, Don and LeAnn decided to cut their empty-nester vacation short. At this point, they were seasoned veterans of both events.

So they left Emily at UNF and headed home to face

what came. While both kids knew about the cancer diagnosis, LeAnn and Don did not belabor the ramifications of it. Both kids were in college, and LeAnn's cancer journey was woven into the fabric of their childhood. LeAnn and Don wanted them to feel as stable as possible, and for that reason they took everything in stride. They didn't allow the diagnosis to dominate their thoughts or emotions, and they moved forward, despite the obvious specter of cancer.

LeAnn underwent surgery in early September 2015, days after the Hurricane Fred nonevent. Dr. H removed the right side of her colon—more than a foot and a half.

Right-sided versus left-sided colon cancer have different implications. If you picture the colon as an inverted "U," the ascending colon, on the right side of our anatomy, is the portion of the colon that connects to the small intestine. So, when doctors remove the right side, as in LeAnn's case, they must also remove the cecum (the portion of the colon that connects to the small intestine); sometimes a part of the ileum (the last section of the small intestine) is also removed. Research shows that patients with right-sided colon cancer have a slightly lower survival rate than those with left-sided cancer. In addition, right-sided colon cancers are considered more aggressive, are more often seen in younger people, and do not respond as well to chemotherapy.

LeAnn's first colon cancer at twenty-nine years old was in the splenic flexure, ironically a left-sided cancer. This is where the transverse colon (the part of the colon that crosses from right to left, or the top of the inverted "U") meets the descending colon, which is why it was hidden from view when the doctors delivered Emily.

Unfortunately, LeAnn's resected bowel caused a condition aptly named "short bowel syndrome," in which there isn't sufficient surface area for adequate digestion. Nobody prepared LeAnn for this complication. She lost fifteen pounds, had little energy, and had to stay close to a bathroom. Through trial and error, she learned high-fiber foods, dairy, and juices were problematic. She couldn't digest high-fiber foods, which led to intestinal blockage. Milk and juice would go straight through her; there was and still is no delay. In those days, drinking juice or milk would send her directly to a bathroom.

Malabsorption (the inability to absorb calories and nutrition) is even more dangerous than the rapid weight loss. Malabsorption leads to undernourishment and vitamin and mineral deficiencies, primarily if part of the ileum is resected. One of the critical deficiencies is vitamin B12. Low B12 leads to tingling of the hands and feet and can cause vision, memory, and balance problems. If left unchecked, it can result in permanent nerve damage or peripheral neuropathy. LeAnn noticed the memory problems the most, and she now receives regular B12 shots.

Other consequences of short bowel syndrome and malabsorption include low iron and poor fluid absorption. The former can cause low energy, depression, breathlessness, tachycardia, and increased infections; the latter causes dehydration and an electrolyte imbalance. These conditions present as nausea, vomiting, confusion, and lethargy. That one resection necessary to save LeAnn's life led to a slew of complications. Each would be addressed, one symptom at a time, until LeAnn's body adjusted, or until she, Don, and her doctors learned the best way to manage the symptoms.

She learned mostly by trial and error—emphasis on the error. For example, one day she made a baked-cauliflower recipe, not considering cauliflower's high fiber content. Needless to say, that was the last time LeAnn ever ate cauliflower.

High-fiber foods especially could cause gastroparesis, or "paralyzed stomach," where the food just stays put. The telltale signs are indigestion and nausea. As soon as this happens, LeAnn only drinks chicken broth until the feeling clears.

Colon cancer surgery is considered a "dirty" surgery. The patient preps and flushes their system as best they can, but it is impossible to entirely clean the digestive tract. Infections are often common, and LeAnn was no exception. After this surgery, LeAnn experienced two infections at the incision site, and it took weeks for the incision to heal.

With each infection, Don had to pack the incision with sterile gauze, pull it out daily, and then repack it with fresh gauze. She took to calling him "Dr. Don," as he did this so she wouldn't have to go to the doctor's office daily.

As this was her first surgery since she and Don had become empty nesters, LeAnn realized she no longer had to hide her suffering or explain the back-and-forth visits to see the surgeon. It was a relief to feel her pain to its fullest and navigate the recovery process without having to frighten her loved ones. Under the care of her trusted teammate, Don, she was able to relax.

God encouraged LeAnn during these times. The only way out was through the trial, and Scripture verses comforted her greatly—especially Psalm 23. Snatches and phrases of it filled her soul: "The Lord is my shepherd; I shall not want... He maketh me to lie down in green pastures... He restoreth my soul... Yea, though I walk through the valley of the shadow of death, I will fear no evil: for thou art with me... Surely goodness and mercy shall follow me all the days of my life: and I will dwell in the house of the Lord forever."

Romans 15:13 also felt like a mainstay: "Now the God of hope fill you with all joy and peace in believing, that ye may abound in hope, through the power of the Holy Ghost." The words would fill her, wash over her and through her, and provide her comfort, peace, and, above all, hope.

In addition to the lengthened healing process and the short bowel syndrome, chemo became an added assault on LeAnn's already traumatized body. It had been nine years since her last chemo in 2007, and this time, there was no "honeymoon phase." It was as if her body recognized the chemo and gave her zero adjustment time.

The oncologist started her with a heavy regimen. She went through two rounds before she was hospitalized for dehydration and vomiting, welcoming 2016 from a hospital bed.

~

Jennifer's Take:

Right around the time I became an empty nester, I started working on this book. When we got to this section, how Don and LeAnn left Emily at college knowing LeAnn would have to go back to face another surgery, I was simply dumbfounded. Now, Jon was in school in town, so they still saw him, but the fear and uncertainty of leaving my daughter while I was facing another surgery would have overwhelmed me. Due to COVID restrictions, my college daughter was at home, taking classes online for the months surrounding my mastectomy, and I remember being grateful that even though there was so much fear and uncertainty, I could face it with my little family all under one roof.

I didn't handle our transition to "empty nester" very easily. It almost felt like nothing prior had prepared my mind for the shock, and the emptiness felt strange and overwhelming. The quiet house almost seemed to vibrate with silence, mocking me. I loved having my girls at home and was fully unprepared for our new phase. Nobody really talks about how difficult it can be, but when I imagined leaving a child at college while I had a cancer diagnosis and surgery looming over me, it hit me hard.

In interviewing LeAnn for this section, I noticed how often she repeated things like, "One step at a time," they would "do the thing." She and Don made a conscious choice to not dwell on the cancer and to not let it branch into every aspect of their lives. They didn't water or tend that diagnosis until it became a giant strangler vine, they simply treated it as a seed—an inconvenient, unfortunate event. What a lesson that became to me. It's so easy to get bad news and allow it to consume me and then to extrapolate all the what-ifs.

LeAnn and Don had learned to take what they were dealt at face value, then they were able to move forward, step by step. In LeAnn's words, they "walk through each door as it's presented." The fear didn't strangle them. They took Philippians 4:8 to heart: "whatsoever things are true, whatsoever things are honest, whatsoever things are pure, whatsoever things are lovely... think on these things."

In contrast, I find the smallest procedures now upend me, and by dwelling on them and traveling down all the potential roads to possible ramifications, I end up making the events much larger than they need to be.

In a few days, I need a minor procedure. I'll be there for an hour and a half, tops. The recovery is minimal. I can even drive myself, which should tell my brain everything it needs to know: No big deal! Yet it feels like such a *big* thing—until I reread this section. And now I've put it in its place: a short inconvenient event that will be over faster than a full-length movie. I'm not going to plant or water that seed. I'm just going to leave it on the table, accepting it at face value. What a freeing feeling! I'm going to do as Philippians 4:8 says and "think on these things." I need to call LeAnn and thank her.

CHAPTER 7

The Struggle Bus

2016

W hile chemo number four wreaked havoc on LeAnn's body, Jon was transitioning from Palm Beach State to Palm Beach Atlantic University (PBA), and Emily had to move back to UNF for the spring semester. Don handled all of it, since between the pain, nausea, dehydration, and hospital stays, LeAnn could not function. Looking back, she can scarcely remember that time.

Once Dr. S. saw LeAnn was not tolerating the original regimen, he pulled back on the cocktail, removing the most problematic drug. LeAnn still refers to it as the "devil part" of the regimen, and her body wanted none of it. After intense nausea, dehydration, and two hospital stays, the doctor changed the regimen, and LeAnn was able to continue. The plan was to stay the course until October.

After five months on this new regimen, though, LeAnn had had enough. There is something called "anticipatory nausea," which happens when you get sick just thinking about what will occur. Xanax (anti-anxiety medication), not Zofran (anti-nausea medication) is the solution, since anticipatory nausea is a psychological phenomenon. One day in May, LeAnn had parked at the oncology building and then realized she had forgotten her Xanax. She sat there, realizing she couldn't get out of the car to submit her body to one more treatment.

As she sat, her car still running, she thought through quitting chemo, what that would mean, and all that would come after it. The faces of her family flashed through her mind—Don, Jon, and Emily. She thought of her future, her children, her husband, parents, and friends.

Then she decided to quit the chemo. The gravity of the decision did not escape her, but the need to walk away and no longer submit to the suffering was too great. The feeling of instant liberation was like nothing she had ever experienced. She could just walk away; she could decide she had had enough.

That was on a Friday. LeAnn came home and told Don, "Let's drive up to Meredith's graduation, because tomorrow I'll be feeling good!" She cried tears of joy. It was a combination of physical and mental relief of kicking chemo in the face—of taking control of her situation and going against the grain.

When LeAnn told her oncologist that she was quitting chemo, he couldn't blatantly agree with her because it went against protocol. But he seemed to understand where she was coming from, he knew what it had done to her. "It's not the standard of care," he said, but he wished her well as she walked out of the office.

Jennifer's Take:

It was a hot April day when I arrived at LeAnn's house for our chemo discussion. She must have heard me pull in because the front door sat ajar, and when I got to the threshold, Lucy, their ten-year-old springer spaniel, greeted me. LeAnn called, "Hello," and the dog led me in. LeAnn smiled weakly, and I observed her heaving chest and puffy face. Today was clearly not a good day.

"Hello, my friend," I said.

"I'm riding the struggle bus today," she said. My heart lifted, because that was LeAnn. Even when she was down, she could spout witty one-liners that drew me to her. They are unique to her, and I wondered afresh who should be writing this book.

We sat quietly after LeAnn told me about quitting chemo, and then I spoke into the silence. "I quit my Tamoxifen, but that's not really the same thing."

Her reply was instant. "Girl, you need to rethink your thinker! It really is the same thing!"

I was duly reprimanded.

Then we sat, the repercussions of our choices vibrating in the air between us.

Tamoxifen is the gold standard treatment for hormone-positive breast cancer. It blocks estrogen and prevents any rogue hormone-positive breast cancer cells from multiplying. The protocol is to take it for at least five years, and most women tolerate it well.

I took it for a year, but at a half dose, and I got breast cancer again. However, with the second breast cancer, we chose a double mastectomy. By this stage, I had had five biopsies, multiple scares, mammograms, ultrasounds, MRIs, and MRI-guided biopsies, and I couldn't even drive by the breast cancer center without feeling my blood pressure rise. The double mastectomy was an easy decision.

But regarding the Tamoxifen, I knew I needed to be on a full dose, and my five-year count had essentially started over. The problem is that Tamoxifen, even at half a dose, made me depressed and irritable. I could feel it "lift" from me about twenty-four hours after I'd taken my daily pill, and it had gotten to the point that if we were going to have a family weekend away, I purposefully wouldn't take it so I could fully enjoy those moments. So, after consulting with my doctors, I had my ovaries removed. Ovaries are a woman's primary source of hormones. From what I understand, removing my ovaries removed ninety-five percent of my hormones, but oncologists still recommend taking Tamoxifen since our bodies have other sources of estrogen production.

I tried. I tried a half dose without the ovaries, and the depression was frightening. I tried an antidepressant, but it gave me a headache and nausea and made me feel like there was a sheet of glass between me and the rest of the world. That's how I felt all day—like I was on one side of the glass, and everyone else was on the other. It was a bizarre sensation. So, I talked it over with my husband, and we decided that my quality of life was more important than the risk. Since both my cancers were Stage 1, and I had removed all the offensive tissue plus the primary source of hormones, we felt I had mitigated my risk.

Neither LeAnn nor I promote stopping any cancer protocol. We simply individually weighed our options and made two very personal decisions. I apologized to my oncologist for stopping my Tamoxifen. I told my doctor I respected the protocol and understood they couldn't condone my choice. I felt like I was letting them down, but I knew I needed to do what was best for me.

I talk to women who have had cancer, and those who stay on the treatment look at me like I have signed a death wish. I wonder if they are tougher than me or have greater mental strength to overcome the adverse side effects. Do they love their families more than I do because they push through despite the adverse effects? It's a conundrum. And then I remember 2 Corinthians 10:12b: "they... comparing themselves among themselves are not wise."

I remember my eldest daughter's response when I discussed stopping my Tamoxifen for the first time. I told her my risk of recurrence without it was less than ten percent. She said, "Mom, if I told you if you walked through that front door, you had a six percent chance of getting your arm chopped off, would you still walk through it?" She had made her point. So, I stayed on the Tamoxifen for another year, but only at the half dose. However, after the recurrence and double mastectomy and oophorectomy, I knew I had lowered my risk further. My husband and I decided together, and I stopped all hormone blockers.

Do I feel sometimes that I gave up and let my daughters down? Yes, sometimes I still do. Do I feel afraid every time I get an odd twinge? Yes, I do. I just had an MRI because of crazy back pain, and thankfully, it was clear, and now I'm seeing a lovely physical therapist who is teaching me back-strengthening exercises, which are already helping alleviate the back pain. I also just had my colonoscopy. I run to my dermatologist and get suspicious bumps frozen or cut off. I see my oncologist every three months and get blood work checking for cancer markers. I'm honest with them, and then I try to put it all out of my mind and enjoy this day, this moment.

I know right now people are reading this and judging— LeAnn for quitting chemo and me for stopping hormone blockers too soon. The fact is it's a personal decision. You weigh whether you want to balance the risk of a higher quality of life with the danger of recurrence. And then you decide, and you allow yourself peace with that decision. Life is short, regardless.

I wake up and tell myself, "Make today count." When beautiful moments happen, I absorb them. I thank God for them. I rest in that moment: a beach walk, a smile from a loved one, a houseful of kids, an orchid that bloomed again, air conditioning, a car that starts every time, music, good food, a great book. There are so many opportunities to enjoy *this moment*. Something about going through hardship elevates those moments. You gain a fresh reason to rejoice; you remember perfect moments are not promised but are gifts from God, and you immerse yourself in them and enjoy them.

Sometimes I wonder why our human psyche is like this. Why did it take prior trauma for me to appreciate the good more fully? Why couldn't I have this realization without the trauma? I'm not sure, but I do know that every good moment is enjoyed more fully than ever before.

When bad times hit, I run back through the good moments, scrolling through my camera roll and allowing myself to reflect on all the good times. Those memories buoy my spirits and remind me God is there no matter the present circumstance.

Only time will tell if our choices were right—or perhaps time won't tell! Nothing is guaranteed except the moment we are in. Worrying about the future or ruminating over the past drains our energy, but rejoicing in the moment we are gifted ensures that today we live with joy and thankfulness no matter our circumstances. Finding joy in the smallest things and taking nothing for granted provides a renewed perspective and peace.

CHAPTER 8

Honor Flights and Elder Care

2016–2020

By May 2016, LeAnn was feeling like herself again, and she hit the ground running. It was summertime, and she could finally enjoy the sun! As an avid sun worshiper and beach lover, enjoying the outdoors felt glorious and gave her a soothing sense of both relief and normalcy.

Her favorite beach was Marcinski Beach, also called Dog Beach, in Juno. She would bring her chair, a beach towel, and a bag with lotion, water bottles, phone, and fresh fruit. And LeAnn would people watch. Others may go to the beach to walk, but her goal was to plant herself, people watch, squish her toes in the sand, and watch the sun reflected off the waves.

LeAnn and Don would also kayak, launching from George Petty Park in West Palm Beach and paddle to the little island called Palmsicle Island. It sits in the Intracoastal, a dot of land due west of Mar-a-Lago.

They had their "poor man's canoe," which Don had sanded and repainted green. He would hoist it onto the pickup truck and pile their inflatable boat into the car along with the dogs, a trolling motor, chairs, and their cooler. They were modern day Beverly Hillbillies once they launched, the trolling motor rigged to the canoe and the inflatable boat holding the cooler and their chairs. They would troll over to the island, inadvertently getting as close to a mansion as permissible. The island, lush with trees, was the perfect spot for the dogs to run. Don and LeAnn would sit and soak in the sun. It was simply beautiful.

One time, though, right after Donald Trump had been elected, they arrived and offloaded as usual. But then they noticed official boats and US marshals approaching, guns visible. They notified the McGraths via loudspeaker they couldn't be nearby when Trump was in town. That was the day the McGraths almost threatened national security.

During that summer, Emily worked at Dollywood in Tennessee. Don and LeAnn decided to surprise both their children. They told Jon (their music guy) that they were visiting Asheville but flew to Nashville instead. The trip was a huge success; Don, LeAnn, and Jon visited every music store in Nashville and then drove to Gatlinburg and surprised Emily.

Once they were all settled in Gatlinburg, Don told the kids to fend for themselves and took LeAnn on a date for a lovely steak dinner while the kids meandered the streets of Gatlinburg. Everybody was happy, and LeAnn let Don know he was nominated for Dad of the Year award again.

With her children graduated from high school, LeAnn had quit working in the cafeteria at TKA and now worked part-time as a CNA. The license allowed her to work as an elder caregiver or companion. In addition, once she had built enough strength to push a wheelchair through the airport, LeAnn started volunteering on honor flights for veterans.

Years before, LeAnn's friend Meg brought LeAnn to an "operation homecoming," which is part of an organization called the Honor Flight Network. Its mission is "To celebrate America's veterans by inviting them to share in a day of honor at our nation's memorials." The nation has over 125 different hubs, and the Southeast Florida Honor Flight hub includes Palm Beach, Martin, and St. Lucie counties.

As LeAnn watched the veterans get off the plane that first time, she felt like a changed person. So many of those soldiers never received a homecoming or the gratitude they deserved for their service. Her own father had been in the Air Force, which had instilled in LeAnn an admiration for all who served. Watching the veterans disembarking to the tune of people cheering, bands playing, and crepe paper decorations and balloons sparked in her a deep desire to give back. That day, LeAnn told herself she would one day be a guardian on an honor flight.

And LeAnn did just that; she went along as a guardian seven times. From the time you leave from Palm Beach International until you fly back in that evening, the entire day focuses on honoring those who have served.

Veterans converge on a Saturday at 4:00 a.m. at Palm Beach International Airport (PBI), where they check in and get their picture taken. Representatives from the army and military are present to welcome them and provide a worthy send-off through a flight gate decorated in red, white, and blue. The veterans board the plane and take off by 6:00 a.m.

As the veterans fly out for Reagan National Airport in Washington, DC, fire trucks line up for a water cannon salute. After they land in DC, they are met by charter buses decorated in red, white, blue, and gold. The volunteers are each assigned a veteran, and they all receive name tags with a sticker that directs them to the appropriate bus.

Their first stop is the Tomb of the Unknown Soldier, where they watch the changing of the guard. Then, they visit either the Iwo Jimo Memorial or the Air Force Memorial, with its three spires pointing into the sky.

A couple of LeAnn's veterans repeated throughout the day, "This is all for me?" LeAnn responded, "Yes, it is, sir. It's all for you!" The volunteers carried their veteran's bags and served them while they ate an Arby's-catered lunch at the armory. During lunch, they would further honor the veterans by announcing the oldest and highest-ranking soldiers, singing patriotic songs, and announcing the corporations that sponsored the day. Every minute of the day was designed to leave an impression that they were being honored.

They spend the afternoon visiting the Korean Memorial, the World War II Memorial, and the Vietnam Wall, where a counselor stands available in case any memory is too overwhelming for our nation's heroes. All seven gentlemen that LeAnn accompanied were Korean war vets.

On the flight home, they provide dinner and a special surprise, something LeAnn said was imperative to be kept secret; she wouldn't even tell me. Their return to the PBI airport is met with fanfare: school bands, family members, and streamers and signs. Our own TKA band played for one of these homecomings.

In addition to the honor flights, LeAnn also worked as a CNA elder companion. She had three primary clients who she took grocery shopping, to eat at restaurants, to doctor's visits, or on walks. Her first client, a man named David, loved to eat at Jetty's and Guanabanas in Jupiter. So, LeAnn would take him to dinner one Saturday a month, and he would tell LeAnn to bring Don along for extra company.

David loved to tell them how, in his younger days, he owned a clothing shop in New York City and only sold the finest clothing. Now that he was retired, his "uniform" was always a solid-colored polo shirt and khaki pants. LeAnn offered to help him buy something different, perhaps something in blue from Lands' End, but he insisted he loved his khakis.

The ladies LeAnn worked with were spunky. They had her grocery shop for them or take them to the salon. One lady loved to eat at Brio at the Garden's Mall, and LeAnn was always happy to take her there.

In the meantime, Jon graduated from college in May 2018. Then he went to Nashville to continue his musical career touring and playing bass guitar with the Alexandra Kay band. The band recently debuted at the Grand Ole Opry. Emily graduated in December 2018 from UNF and again recently with a master's degree in counseling from Liberty University and now works as an elementary school counselor in North Florida.

With their kids settled into rewarding careers, life ran on autopilot. LeAnn continued to work with her elderly clients and go on as many honor flights as their budget would allow. Although her body never recovered from the radiation, and her shortened bowels gave her difficulty, "normal" had returned. She recognized every day was a gift, and she lived it with gusto. Her primary motivation was always looking for others to help and encourage.

Jennifer's Take:

I think back to the times I was the recipient of LeAnn's mission to help others. LeAnn delivered a large dose of encouragement every time I called her, especially before my double mastectomy. LeAnn lived out these beautiful verses from Isaiah 58:7 and undoubtedly received the reward promised in verse eight:

> "Is it not to deal thy bread to the hungry,
>   and that thou bring the poor that are
>   cast out to thy house? When thou seest
>   the naked, that thou cover him; and that
>   thou hide not thyself from thine own
>   flesh?
> Then shall thy light break forth as the morn-

ing, and thine health shall spring forth
speedily: and thy righteousness shall go
before thee; the glory of the LORD shall
be thy reward."

Our light shall "break forth as the morning." What an
apt depiction of light piercing the darkness, and it is
promised to those who help others!

Another woman who was touched by LeAnn's kindness
was Anne, a coworker and friend. In her late forties, in the
middle of what Anne had always gratefully considered a
"charmed life," Anne discovered her husband of twenty-five
years was having an affair. He ultimately chose to leave Anne
and their four children, and their divorce was finalized on
Anne's fiftieth birthday.

Only six months later, still reeling from the heartbreak
and shock, one of Anne's teen daughters became ill. Her
traumatic ten-month hospitalization, long-term rehabilita-
tion, and subsequent kidney transplant surgery filled the
months until Anne turned fifty-two. On Thanksgiving Day
of that same year, Anne's mother was suddenly hospitalized
and did not recover. She was gone before Christmas.

The following year, Anne began to have unusual symptoms of her own. After doctor's visits, tests, periods of igno-
rance, and then more tests, she was finally diagnosed with
Parkinson's Disease.

Amid all these "big things" were many other ordinary
life "big things," like kids going to college, parents needing
assistance, financial struggles, and of course, the isolation

and disruption of a global pandemic. "Suffice it to say, on some days these past ten years, I have questioned God's plan, and I have not wanted to get out of bed to see what the next day had in store," Anne said.

However, she would also say she still lived a "charmed life." When people ask how that's possible, her answer is "community." Throughout these periods of crisis, she was blessed to be the receiver of the prayers, sacrifice, and offerings of the community of Christians in which God had so providentially placed her.

Some were true miracles. The husband of a fellow teacher stepped forward with faith, knowing God was telling him to act, and became the perfect kidney match for her daughter.

Other provisions were simple and unexpected. Anne was also a teacher at The King's Academy. During Anne's marital disintegration, while barely holding the responsibilities of work and children together, leftover boxed sandwiches would somehow make their way to Anne's classroom. The kids loved those egg-salad sandwiches, and Anne felt a burden lifted every time a leftover box arrived in her classroom.

Those sandwiches were evidence that God was meeting her needs. She was too tired to cook, too strapped to face the grocery store, and there, sitting in her classroom was evidence that God's people saw her need and cared. God's people made Matthew 6:26 ring true, the promise more poignant: "Behold the fowls of the air: for they sow not, neither do they reap, nor gather into barns; yet your heavenly Father feedeth them. Are ye not much better than they?"

So, although the song Anne sings is often a "Broken Hallelujah," she still believes she has been given a "charmed life." It has been filled to the brim with the love, care, and fellowship of God's people. "I have learned," Anne said, "that when the next inevitable 'big thing' comes, God will always provide a lunch lady."

But here's the kicker: I sent this piece to LeAnn for her approval, and she never told me the rest of the story. It was only after resending edits to Anne that she wrote back: "I suppose you have figured out by now who the lunch lady was?"

My mouth dropped open. I should have known!

LeAnn was the lunch lady, because that is who LeAnn is: Someone who quietly stays behind the scenes and helps others. She was helping me while adjusting to her ostomy bag. She was going on honor flights honoring veterans when money was tight, and she probably should have been spoiling herself. She was delivering food to Anne's room when she was tired after a long day on her feet in the cafeteria. I imagine her list of helps is too long for this book.

I also know LeAnn will never admit to them all, so we will let her keep her secrets and smile to ourselves, our hearts warming with the understanding that LeAnn is a gift to everyone who knows her.

In prior conversations, LeAnn admitted what has become starkly evident: Her greatest joy comes in finding ways to help people. When my own daughter was sick, she came to my house and sat with her so I could go on a paddle boarding.

This makes her work with the veterans and as a CNA even more poignant. Sometimes LeAnn's current state precludes this work, and that makes her sad. Yet, when I went through my breast cancers, she spent hours on the phone with me talking through my options. I always hung up feeling like I had just left the best counseling session available on earth. My heart would lift; my spirits would lighten. All because LeAnn, despite the pain and suffering she endured, was looking outward and living out Isaiah 58:8.

CHAPTER 9

Cancer #5

2020

In January 2020, LeAnn went in for her yearly colonoscopy. The doctors discovered a precancerous "lesion" and informed her it needed to be removed along with what remained of her colon; there simply was not enough healthy colon left for another resection. Her irradiated pelvis had left her remaining colon like tissue paper, too diseased to save.

The solution, to remove the colon entirely, made sense, but at the time LeAnn had no inkling of the ramifications of living without a colon. LeAnn and Don met with three surgeons hoping to communicate how damaged her pelvic area was; the surgeon needed to be comfortable with what would be a complex surgery.

They finally settled on Dr. D at the Weston Cleveland Clinic. Dr. D removed LeAnn's remaining colon and part of her small intestine and connected an ileostomy bag to her small intestine. This differs from a colostomy bag, which is connected to a patient's large intestine or colon.

Before LeAnn's surgery, the doctor gave her the option to have either a reversible or a permanent bag placed. LeAnn and Don went back and forth in their decision-making, but on the day of the surgery, they told the surgeon to make it a permanent bag; she knew she would battle liquid output for the rest of her life. To this day, despite the trauma of the chaotic adjustment period, Don and LeAnn know it was the right choice.

Only six short weeks passed between the colonoscopy and surgery. However, by then, that precancerous lesion was now full-blown cancer. Her four-and-a-half-year cancer reprieve had ended.

After the surgery, LeAnn was in the ICU for three days before spending the remainder of a week in a step-down then a regular room. The surgery happened on March 2, 2020, at the same time a disease called COVID was causing increasing alarm. A week later, the administration was actively locking down the hospital.

The evening of her discharge, LeAnn sat in in a line of wheelchairs waiting to be let out. Security guards stood at the doors, preventing anyone from entering. They went from door to door, keys jangling, locking every entrance. It felt like something out of a horror movie, and she watched from her wheelchair, still so sick, her surgery fresh, the bag attached to her side.

Perhaps due to COVID, LeAnn was unprepared for life with an ileostomy bag. The world outside was changing, and hospitals were postponing routine surgeries and using their facilities to treat COVID patients instead.

Before LeAnn's release, the nurse entered and delivered a hurried tutorial on ileostomy care. The nurse gave LeAnn and Don parameters and instructions, but their heads were buzzing. They had no clue what was going on. They gleaned what they could, took the offered pamphlets, and winged it from there. The thought was that eventually her small intestine would take over the job of the colon, but LeAnn's irradiated pelvis was probably more damaged than they realized.

They needed an on-call nurse—someone to come to their house and offer hands-on, in-depth assistance for at least the first two weeks. But with COVID, no help was available. They were on their own. And as LeAnn sat in that line of wheelchairs, waiting, the tidal wave of what faced them loomed ahead.

The first weeks at home were a nightmare. LeAnn would sit and feel liquid spewing out of her. Her body would not absorb anything, and there was zero regulation. Fluid in meant fluid out—violently. Anything she ate or drank poured directly into her bag. She was in the bathroom every thirty minutes. Her bag holds 500 mL, and she could dump as much as 5000 mL daily. Even though LeAnn's ostomy bag is a "high output" bag, her body's output was too high, and her electrolytes were washed out. With each spew of liquid, there went her magnesium, sodium, water—everything. They had no clue how to manage, and everything was a blur. The pamphlets she had been sent home with were zero help.

Within four days after discharge, LeAnn was readmitted

and spent ten days at Palms West Hospital in Royal Palm Beach for dehydration. The doctors would give her bag after bag of hydration to replenish what she had lost, but it would come straight out.

Palms West sent her home after ten days, and by April 10, LeAnn was so severely dehydrated she was admitted to Good Samaritan Hospital. By then, her doctor had prescribed Lomotil, a medication to slow her output.

By the middle of May, LeAnn was down thirty pounds, lethargic, and malnourished. Thankfully, Dr. S decided to supplement LeAnn with Total Parenteral Nutrition (TPN) and hydration. TPN is considered complete replacement nutrition via IV and contains lipid emulsions, dextrose, amino acids, electrolytes, vitamins, minerals, and trace elements. The doctors started TPN with a Peripherally Inserted Central Catheter (PICC) line, hoping the TPN would be temporary. A PICC line is more durable than an IV and accesses larger veins. But PICC lines generally have a life of less than six months, and LeAnn had multiple PICC line infections and a total of four lines placed. Coupled with the realization that the TPN would need to last for the fore-seeable future, the doctors eventually placed a central line. LeAnn was given two lines—one for hydration and one for her TPN.

For the first five days, her TPN ran for twenty-four hours a day— until her bloodwork was regulated—and then they reduced her TPN to eighteen hours a day. They tried to lower it to twelve hours daily, but her blood work wasn't ideal, so they brought her back to sixteen hours every day.

Despite careful planning and monitoring, LeAnn has been admitted to Good Samaritan twenty-six times in the last three years because of central line infections or dehydration.

Recently, LeAnn also learned her thyroid hormone is low, and her new endocrinologist, Dr. F, is managing this. Adding thyroid hormone to her three years of ostomy education has brought her to a precarious balance on days when she is well enough to leave the house.

Now when LeAnn looks back to those first days with the ostomy bag, she realizes they had zero concept of what was involved. Prior to the surgery, she felt relieved because she would no longer have to deal with short bowel syndrome and the urgent, associated pain of acid coming straight through. She thought the bag meant the urgency would go away, but she never realized those same contents would simply transfer to the bag.

Due to COVID restrictions during all LeAnn's hospital admissions, Don was not allowed in. LeAnn had to learn to do everything on her own. She needed someone at her bedside, but the medical personnel were tapped out. Whether because of COVID or poor training, the healthcare professionals did not seem to understand ostomy care; they treated it (and as a by-product, LeAnn) as foreign and gross, and they were unsure how to react. At one time, LeAnn remembered emptying and changing the bag while a healthcare person stood at a distance, watching. Finally, in exasperation, LeAnn looked at them and said, "You are not going to get sprayed, but I could use an extra hand." She needed Don; he knew how to help, and he wasn't disgusted by her bag.

LeAnn now has a two-piece bag with a wafer attached to her belly. The stoma, the part of the small intestine surgically attached to the opening in her abdomen, sticks out and connects to the wafer. Then, the bag opening matches the wafer. She can either empty the bag or put a whole new bag on. She also changes the wafer every three to five days, but this involves removing adhesive and then using glue and a hairdryer to dry it before she replaces the wafer. Originally, it would take LeAnn an hour to change it, but now, at home with Don's help, they can change that wafer in five minutes!

LeAnn now knows what foods to avoid and has her own personal "nope" list: mushrooms and spinach don't digest, cauliflower is out, corn can cause a blockage, acidic foods are off the table, and she avoids sweets because sugar comes through too fast. The learning curve was sharp and brutal, and those first six months were a blur. She felt like they were chasing their tails, trying to stay ahead of the bag. If the bag got too full, it would bulge off her belly. She felt like a newborn mom without a clue. Before a trip anywhere, she would empty the bag right before they left. Yet, no matter their preparation, they would find themselves stuck. So, they started traveling with supplies.

It probably took LeAnn a year to adjust to "her," AKA the bag, which LeAnn insists "shall not be named." In everything, they have found the overwhelming positive: LeAnn can no longer get colon cancer unless her body decides to recognize her small intestine as a colon and place colon cancer there. She has come to terms with the fact that she can control the bathroom. She can travel again, always prepared with supplies.

The comorbidities LeAnn contends with every day—in her own ironic words—"truly stink." She has had to remain on TPN for nutrition. She must stay hydrated, drink often, and add a hydration bag when output is too high. The central line associated with her TPN requires sterile procedures and constant vigilance. Sterile procedures are second nature to her and Don.

Despite their caution, anytime LeAnn has a fever, she must go to the hospital so they can draw cultures and determine if the line has become compromised. To date, LeAnn has gone septic four times, has had six lines (counting this newest one) placed in her chest, one in the groin, and has had four PICC lines.

Yet, through it all, LeAnn has come to terms with "her." The bag will always be a part of her. On rare occasions, when LeAnn thinks she would like to have a reversal, she remembers how bad that life was and comes to her senses.

Even though you can swim with ostomy bags, LeAnn can't swim with a central line. She also still deals with blockages. They start with an uncomfortable pain in her upper abdomen due to intestinal spasms, then persistent nausea follows, and the thought of eating feels abhorrent. When this happens, LeAnn drinks water or sips broth, but does not eat, until the output lets her know that the blockage has cleared. The TPN provides her nutrition, so she no longer needs to be hospitalized for a blockage. NG tubes are thankfully a thing of the past.

Don will offer to eat outside on the days LeAnn can't eat, but she won't hear of that. He has sacrificed too much for her, so she insists he sit with her and enjoy his food.

Jennifer's Take:

The ostomy adjustment months coincide with the phone calls where LeAnn counseled me through both of my breast cancers. There are tears in my eyes as I write this, and I feel incredibly humbled. I never knew, but now I realize LeAnn never wanted me to know.

This realization takes me back to her desire to help others. LeAnn focusses on others; she looks outward instead of inward, and this inspires me to look around and do the same.

Easter morning comes, and the overwhelming joy of the resurrection washes over me. LeAnn had been on my heart throughout the weekend. At the time of writing this, I know it's her wedding anniversary, and she wishes her circumstances could be different. I wonder if her nausea has calmed down. I pray she hasn't experienced any blockages. I hope she is well enough to enjoy the Easter weekend and their anniversary without all the extras piling on and sapping her of energy and joy.

The hope of what Easter means to me and LeAnn settles over me. We don't have to have perfect scenarios. We may not get that ideal result here on earth, but eternity is just that: eternal. LeAnn has a glorious eternity awaiting her.

But still, I am uncomfortable. I want LeAnn to experience joy and good health and her favorite things today. Right now, here on earth. I want to tell God she has suffered enough and to allow her this weekend to be one of pure joy.

Then I recall the Hebrews 11 martyrs—those who made it to the Hebrews Hall of Fame but still died for their faith. The martyrs didn't have less faith than those who experienced earthly victory. They *all* had faith. Our modern Christianity would probably ascribe those who saw earthly victory as having "more faith," but that is not what the Scriptures tell us. They *all* had faith—so much faith they are all considered Heroes of the Faith.

And I think about LeAnn and what she endures every single day. I know she is a hero of the faith—not because she can look back on what she endured and has emerged on the other side, but because she knows her hope is in God, no matter the discouragement and the pain. LeAnn knows and clings to the fact that He is her enduring hope. And, because of the resurrection, because He rose again, we can face today and tomorrow. So, instead, I pray that if Easter is a difficult day for her, the truth of the resurrection will fill her heart and soul with joy.

CHAPTER 10

Hurt people hurt people

A BACKWARD LOOK

T he first eight years of LeAnn's life were spent in a small, white two-bedroom, one-bath house in Fort Lauderdale. LeAnn's dad had a successful career in law enforcement. But his success was tempered by alcohol and a troubled childhood, which certainly colored LeAnn's upbringing. Her mom, who stayed home with LeAnn for a season, later worked as an administrative assistant. As detailed in chapter one, her mom also struggled with addiction.

LeAnn's parents divorced when LeAnn was eight, and she lived with her mother for five years until her father married her stepmom, Joanne. Once she reached thirteen, LeAnn began alternating between households—each fraught with difficulty, and neither a haven for a growing teen. LeAnn wasn't a good student, and her dad and stepmom were tough on her. Because her grades were poor, she was always on restriction, so she spent most of those months in her room. She remembers being disciplined, eating dinner with them, and doing the dishes. There wasn't much dialogue and zero companionship, which compounded the difficulty of deciding which parent deserved her loyalty and which parent would be more physically and emotionally supportive. Her dad, still battling alcoholism, was harsh with her, and her mom was self-absorbed, dealing with prescription drug addiction. LeAnn didn't have anybody she trusted—no go-to person.

After a restriction-filled seventh grade year, she moved back in with her mom for eighth grade, then returned to her dad's house for ninth and tenth grades and, once again, spent her time on restriction. She yo-yoed back and forth between her parents, constantly choosing what seemed to her youthful mind as the lesser of the two evils. Her dad's house felt more stable, but the restrictions and lack of companionship wore thin. Her mom's house had companionship, but the continual uncertainty from living with an addict made her miss the regimented life at her dad's house.

A bright spot in the back-and-forth dilemma between houses was LeAnn's childhood summers spent in Land O'Lakes, Florida, with her maternal grandparents. Besides signing LeAnn up for swim lessons and visiting their friends' houses, LeAnn's grandparents would take her to political meetings once a week. She remembers sitting in the back with her cousin, swinging her legs from the hard plastic chairs, a little elephant insignia pin on her T-shirt. She doesn't remember anything about the meetings, only that she was a kid at a grown-up meeting and had to stay quiet.

In addition to the political meetings, she watched the news and then, at seven p.m., Lawrence Welk each evening with her grandpa. There was comfort in routine.

Her grandparents were devout believers and belonged to the local Methodist church. One afternoon toward the end of the summer, LeAnn clearly remembers the pastor coming over to the house to visit with them; the pastor told her about Jesus's love. He explained in a way that connected with her eight-year-old mind the way Jesus loved her and died for her. Despite attending Sunday School and church, she had never heard God's love broken down like this, and for the first time she understood this was a decision she could make for herself. She knew a lot about Jesus because of her private school and church, but up until that point she had never realized she could *know* Jesus.

LeAnn was baptized that Sunday. She was only eight, and although her parents were already separated, they both made the trip for the baptism. She felt nervous and realizes now there was unnecessary pressure, and she complied more out of a need to keep the adults in her life satisfied than for any other reason. She felt more peaceful after praying with the pastor and getting baptized, but she doesn't remember if her happiness came from satisfying the adults or because she genuinely did have a sense of peace.

As an older teen, LeAnn rededicated her commitment to God. At this point, she realized her decision was wholly hers, and she believed deep in her heart that Jesus was who he said he was, and she prayed in earnest. John 14:6 illuminated her thoughts and her prayers: "I am the way, the truth and the life: no man cometh unto the Father, but by me."

At the end of her tenth grade year, her mom planned a vacation to Kansas City. Her dad refused to let LeAnn go due to bad grades. In response, LeAnn moved back in with her mom and stayed with her until high school graduation. This move necessitated a new high school, which turned out to be a positive development. LeAnn joined the swim team (swimming backstroke) and formed solid friendships with her teammates.

At the beginning of eleventh grade, she also began working at Publix, Florida's biggest grocery chain, and continued working there through high school graduation and during her months of EMT school.

LeAnn's father is eighty now, and she struggles to visit him. Prior to her ostomy surgery, she went and stayed with him frequently, but now she can't be there for him, and this is difficult for her. Joanne, his second wife, died in April 2019 from early-onset Alzheimer's, and not long after that, her dad had open heart surgery. LeAnn spent seven weeks in Sebastian helping him. However, since the March 2020 ostomy surgery, she can no longer assist him. Despite this, they video chat often and her dad now spends his retirement days restoring fishing rods and reels.

Her mother was more local but stayed in an assisted living facility. She was difficult to visit for different reasons, so LeAnn stuck to Mother's Day, Thanksgiving, and Christmas. It was a complicated relationship. LeAnn wanted to respect and provide for her mom, but the lifetime of addiction and manipulation hovered beneath the surface.

LeAnn's mom passed away on May 29, 2023. LeAnn had ample warning, and she was able to go back and forth to see her mom. She had some guilt over not being sad enough. It was difficult mourning her mom—not necessarily for her passing, but for what could have and should have been. Addiction alters lives, often irrevocably, and it marked her childhood.

Jennifer's Take:

When LeAnn walked into my house the day we discussed her parents, I could tell she was worn out. I got her seated, propped her feet up, refilled her ice water, and waited.

She took a deep breath and explained she planned to visit her dad. He lives in Sebastian, and that means a drive and an overnight stay. I could tell the anticipation was draining her.

"Is there any way you can just not go?" I asked.

"Girl, I planned this. My Dad is eighty. I need to see him."

I nodded. Of course. Their love for each other is palpable. I've been present for two random video chats, and the joy there has warmed my heart. Her dad has overcome so much and is an example of how it is never too late to live free of past addiction.

Tears coursed down LeAnn's cheeks. This was the first

time in all our conversations that I'd seen her cry. It broke my heart.

The conversation about her dad inevitably lead to her mom.

"You can forgive the past and move on from it, but when negative memories return, I just have to remind myself that hurt people hurt people."

The truth in her words hit me hard.

"But LeAnn, you broke the cycle," I tried, wanting to provide comfort. "You are not your mom. You have endured so much, yet everyone wants to be your friend. Your children love you; your husband is still your valentine. You broke the cycle of addiction and poor relationships, despite what you have lived and are living through. Can you hear the crowds cheering? You belong in Hebrews eleven. I picture God looking down with His hand on your shoulder. He is saying, 'You, my child, are a hero. I love you.'"

She tilted her head. "Well, that's what you see. I don't know. I did not start out as a good mom. I was too short tempered. I had high expectations. I made a lot of mistakes."

"But we all make mistakes," I countered. "The difference is, we apologize for those mistakes."

"Yes, I have apologized for my mistakes," she admitted. "By the time my kids were in late middle school, I stepped back. I just loved them. Then we had great years. I was their number-one cheerleader. I got better at the parenting thing as the kids got older. I hope they recognize that."

I sat there and realized LeAnn has accepted her childhood for what it was. She is not bitter, and I realized afresh how she has broken the cycle. While we talked, her phone kept pinging. It was her kids, her dad, and Don, all trying to figure out the logistics of a family group chat. Emily had recently been nominated for Rookie Teacher of the Year, and Jon was touring in Brisbane, Australia, fourteen hours ahead. They had much to discuss!

This is tangible evidence of how LeAnn broke the cycle. Her children are in touch, her dad wants to chat with her, and her husband will be home soon, ready to install their new washing machine. The family has taken LeAnn's illness in stride, and they love their mom, daughter, and wife. It's beautiful.

Our media-induced notion of romance is a movie or reel with beautiful people in perfect settings falling in love. But the true love story played out right before me. And that love expands and moves in and around the trial and heartache that TPN and infected lines and cancer have brought.

I want to bottle up this love LeAnn's family has for each other and share it with the world. I want my words to convey that what I see before me is unique but possible for others, no matter their trials. Love doesn't require perfection; love and happiness can coexist with pain and suffering. I feel honored to be there and to witness it all.

Recently, LeAnn shared a song with me called "The Apple" by Makena Hartlin. The song is all about breaking the cycle and writing your own life far from addiction or alcoholism, or whatever you were dealt as a child. Find it on YouTube and give it a listen.

CHAPTER 11

Widen Those Veins

I n early July, 2023, LeAnn's home healthcare nurse began struggling to draw blood from her line. He talked to her GI doctor, who set her up with Dr. Z, an interventional radiologist. Dr. Z diagnosed the problem: Superior Vena Cava Syndrome, or SVC. It's a clotting disease and, translated into lay terms, means the superior vena cava, the vein that carries blood away from the upper body, is partially blocked with clots. It's the reason LeAnn's face had become increasingly puffy.

In addition, Dr. Z explained that LeAnn's veins and arteries were too narrow and would need stents. The plan was to go in and remove the existing central lines, clean up the area, stretch her veins with a balloon, and place stents. Then LeAnn would have to stay on blood thinners for the rest of her life.

The central line would unfortunately need to be moved to the groin area. This thought obviously horrified LeAnn.

Nobody wants nutrition to go into that area; it feels wrong. Dr. Z promised LeAnn he would place an extension onto it so the ports would rest on her belly. That way, they could attach the feeding tube at this juncture, and LeAnn wouldn't have to feel embarrassed when her home healthcare nurse came to check her lines.

Thank goodness for small victories.

The procedure would happen in two steps, and LeAnn needed to be in the ICU for part of it. The surgery ended up being quite extensive. The doctor cleared all the veins in her neck and leading into her arms. LeAnn was sore, and the undersides of her arms were black and blue from where the doctor stretched her veins. But she immediately lost nine pounds, the equivalent of over a gallon of water. The puffiness in her face went away.

LeAnn was given one line with a Y-tube splitting off, mimicking her old double line. At the end of her hospital bed was a stand with six monitors and four IV bags—enough convolution to launch a spaceship. Despite all this, once they deemed her stable enough, she was sent home.

Prior to the surgery, the doctor said after LeAnn's chest area had rested, they could go back and put the port into her chest. After the surgery, he said it might not ever be possible again. The proclamation felt ominous, like LeAnn was running out of options. If she no longer had a spot for her port, she couldn't receive TPN and would starve. Someone at some point had told her she would only last a few days without it. Suddenly, the end felt nearer than it ever had, and LeAnn left unsettled and heartbroken. She wasn't ready for an "end;" there was still too much life left to live. She and Don are a team, and the thought of leaving him was unconscionable.

~

Jennifer's Take:

I'll never forget the day LeAnn told me about her SVC diagnosis. I was driving over a bridge to the beach to meet a friend, and LeAnn's words contrasted sharply with my view. Crystal-blue water rushed beneath me—incoming tide, the perfect time to snorkel and paddle. Boats, swimmers, and paddleboarders moved about, all healthy enough to embrace the stunning South Florida day. The contrast pulled at my mind, made worse by LeAnn's love of the sunshine and water. I often wonder how it feels to sit at home and know a simple day in the salt, sand, and sun is impossible.

I forced myself back to our conversation.

"Remember when you said the book was too short?" LeAnn was saying.

I tried to laugh, still trying to juxtapose the surrounding view with this latest news.

"Well, now we have a new chapter."

My heart sank. We didn't need a new chapter that badly.

"It's because my arteries have blood clots, that's why my face is so puffy."

. . .

After the surgery, they discharged her directly from the ICU to home.

"We can take it from here, Dr. Don and I," she said. "I'm stable enough, and we know what to do." Don and LeAnn are surgery recovery veterans, and Don needs to be awarded an honorary MD. They are an amazing couple; LeAnn is determined to not be a bother, and Don can manage whatever comes their way. He is simultaneously nurse, doctor, and husband. As someone who loves reading a good love story, I know I'm watching one unfold right before me. This is love.

A few days post-surgery, I received this exact text:

"Today has not been such a great day. So, I'm just going to settle in with my ice water and maybe a cookie around 8 o'clock or so. I just can't hardly get out of my own head today. I'm not quite sure why. We'll chalk it up to post-anesthesia brain."

I called her immediately. "Are you having a hard time with this?"

It is only the second time in all our talks that I could hear her crying. My heart broke. "It's completely understandable," I said. "Plus, all of this is brand new and something you have no prior knowledge of, so it's got to be overwhelming."

"Yes," she said. "It's just that I feel like I'm running out of options. I mean, nobody is telling me I'm going to die or anything, but if I run out of places to get nutrition, then…

"And now I have to be on blood thinners for the rest of my life, and my skin is going to get that look to it, you know, with the pinpricks? But that takes years to develop, and I am already fifty-seven, so I guess it won't matter if, in my sixties, you see skin marks, right? I mean, why am I being vain about this anyway?"

LeAnn, with Don by her side, has been through so much. And sometimes, it just gets to be too much. She's allowed to be human.

"You were in the ICU a few minutes ago," I tried, "so why not let yourself do nothing? You don't have to accomplish anything today or tomorrow or the next day until your veins stop hurting. You've earned the right to do nothing."

Why do we feel we must "accomplish" even after a major medical event? Permitting ourselves to heal is vital. I'll never forget asking my surgeon post-mastectomy if I could return to work after four weeks off rather than six weeks.

He looked at me and smiled and said something that gave me that unspoken permission I needed to heal: "You can't rush tissue healing." he said. "It doesn't matter your mindset; the body has a physiological need to take a certain amount of time to heal. You can try to rush it, but then you'll land up back in my office, infected and needing even more time off."

I want to repeat this to LeAnn, but I know she knows it. Plus, I've learned when I don't know what to say, I ought to stop trying. Sometimes it's better to say nothing.

CHAPTER 12

God's Chicken

O n LeAnn's most recent visit to the oncologist, she had her blood tested for cancer markers. The bloodwork includes the CA 27-29 and CEA markers, which both provide evidence of cancer recurrence. Because LeAnn has had uterine cancer, her oncologist also checks her CA-125 levels, which, if elevated, can be evidence of recurring uterine cancer. The blood tests are not definitive, but a warning light.

On that latest visit, her CA-125 was over triple what it should be.

Those markers had always been within range for her, even when she had cancer. So, if the marker was that high, did that mean the cancer was everywhere?

The doctors wanted to do a CT scan or a PET (positron emission tomography) scan, but LeAnn couldn't hold the CT contrast in her body; it drained straight into her ostomy bag. So, it would have to be a PET scan, but it would be hard to get insurance approval.

The scenarios started to stack in LeAnn's head. She couldn't have more GI surgery since she had no colon and a shortened intestine. She couldn't do chemo again since she was on TPN and would never survive the onslaught. She was on blood thinners to prevent clots, which precludes most surgeries. The list ended in the fear that this, whatever "this" now was, was her final straw.

LeAnn received her approval for a PET scan, and it was scheduled for Wednesday, August 23, 2023.

Since a PET scan involves injecting radioactive glucose into the patient, the prep means no sugars for twenty-four hours prior. Cancer cells take up glucose faster than other cells, so the radioactive glucose would highlight any areas where cancer is present. Eating sugar prior to the test would skew the results.

So, LeAnn's Tuesday diet included two pieces of fish and not much else. She couldn't have her usual TPN and hydration, since both contained sugars. She was so lethargic, she wasn't sure how she was going to make it until her procedure. The morning of, I stayed on the phone with her chatting about nothing, trying to distract her.

Right before we disconnected, she said, "God is answering my prayers. I blinked, and the clock went from ten to eleven!"

But when she arrived for the procedure, the insurance had denied it. It was escalated to "mandatory" for approval within forty-eight hours. But LeAnn didn't know why she'd been scheduled if it hadn't been approved.

On the way home they stopped and got some "God's chicken," which is what LeAnn calls Chick-fil-A. LeAnn maintained that God's chicken could fix a world of woes, and for the short term, she could stay in the dark and not have to receive a new diagnosis.

Jennifer's Take:

When LeAnn called me to tell me she had arrived ready for the PET scan and was denied, I was horrified. I felt myself shriveling up—then I realized if I was this fearful, angry, and sad, I couldn't imagine the scale of LeAnn's fear, disappointment, despair, and trepidation.

We have already planned a visit, and now I was determined to let nothing stand in the way. I needed to see her in person. I needed to hug her and give her daisies and make her smile.

We are not promised easy lives, but we are promised an eternity in heaven. LeAnn has not had an easy life. LeAnn's life is the antithesis of everything I see when I scroll through Instagram.

But LeAnn has an enduring hope. Her hope is in Jesus, the anchor of her soul. And when I feel sad or down or depressed that LeAnn may not get her healing on earth, I picture her stepping into the arms of Jesus and Him saying to her, "Well done." I imagine her swimming in the celestial sea and laughing with the saints who have gone before her.

I picture joy.

CHAPTER 13

Right as Rain

I n September, LeAnn landed back in the hospital with severe dehydration. When she arrived, her systolic pressure (the top number) was sixty-two. She couldn't even walk to the bathroom on her own.

The IV fluids helped immediately, and their instant thought was LeAnn would have to add a daily hydration bag at the end of the sixteen hours of TPN. The hours of "freedom" from being attached keep shrinking. Even though her small intestine should have taken over the job of the colon by now, it had not complied. She simply did not absorb enough water.

While admitted, her doctor planned a CT scan in place of the failed PET ordeal. The doctor said they could have her drink the contrast and then go immediately into the machine before her body spewed it back out.

What a nightmare.

That rehydration hospital stay turned out to be nearly two weeks long.

Whenever LeAnn went into the hospital, the doctors ran cultures on her central line to ensure it was not infected. On the first and second day, the cultures come back positive. They began IV antibiotics to try to save the new line—the fancy new groin one placed only on July 18.

By day three, despite their best efforts, LeAnn went septic. She turned gray, she couldn't stop shaking, and her fever spiked. The rapid response team swooped in. Her mean arterial pressure (MAP), something doctors want to be at least sixty-five, hovered in the fifties. They moved her to the ICU. Saving the permanent line was now out of the question, and the doctor removed it, placing a temporary line in the left groin.

There was not time to put LeAnn to sleep—she was critical—so everything happened while she was awake. This was a first. As soon as they'd secured the replacement line, the doctor explained she was about to pull the old, infected one. For LeAnn, this felt like the final straw. She did not want more pain, and she lost her mind. It was too much.

Another line.

Another rapid response.

The ICU.

Sepsis.

More pain.

The doctor promised it wouldn't feel like much, and the nurse held her hand. And in one millisecond, the doctor pulled that beautifully-placed-but-now-infected line.

"It's out?" LeAnn asked. "It's out, and I didn't feel hardly anything?"

The doctor smiled and nodded, and LeAnn felt so happy and relieved that it felt like a birthday party in the ICU.

Eventually, LeAnn rallied and graduated back to a regular room where she was able to hold onto the contrast long enough for a successful CT scan.

The CT came back clean—no evidence of tumors. Her oncologist reminded LeAnn that elevated tumor markers can happen for reasons besides cancer. Given LeAnn's history and the fact that despite five other cancers, hers had never been elevated, the fear had been valid. Yet, after the recent sepsis, relief felt anticlimactic. Such are the ups and downs of the life of a cancer survivor.

Her interventional radiologist, Dr. Z—the doctor who placed the groin line in July—stopped by to check her temporary line. He told LeAnn the CT scan had provided double duty, showing him there were no apparent clots. The blood thinner, Eloquis, was working! LeAnn could once again get a line placed in her chest. What a gift!

LeAnn headed home from the hospital on IV antibiotics to await the procedure at JFK North to get another line in her chest. The line would be placed as an outpatient, but it would be painful. LeAnn was afraid Dr. Z was wrong, afraid the line couldn't be placed, afraid there were still clots. And if they couldn't place that line, then what? No line meant no nutrition, and she didn't even want to think about no nutrition meant.

The morning of the procedure, as they drove to JFK North, Don asked LeAnn if she was nervous. This time, she was exceedingly so. Given the last few months, it felt surreal that Dr. Z would be able to find a spot.

Don's words were simple and exactly what she needed to hear: "If anyone can find a spot, he can. Remember, he told you when you were in the hospital for sepsis that you are so much better off than you were in July?"

And just like that, LeAnn felt better. Don always knew what to say.

Dr. Z was able to place that line in her chest. He gave her a single lumen, or single line, rather than a double lumen. With a double line, one line is used for TPN and the other for hydration, meds, and any blood draws. The single line prevented him from stretching the vein, and LeAnn adjusted. He placed a splitter, a Y-shaped tube, on the single line so they can still hook up her hydration along with the TPN. The pain was gone from the procedure, and the line was behaving as it should.

Not long afterwards, LeAnn went in for her cardiology follow-up, and her cardiologist couldn't believe how her puffiness had subsided. The cardiologist managed one of LeAnn's latest diagnoses: POTS, or postural orthostatic tachycardia syndrome.

POTS has gained increasing attention in the post-COVID era. Patients experience rapid heart rate when standing and become lightheaded and dizzy. In severe cases, patients may faint multiple times per day. Blood pools in the legs and feet when sitting, and the body does not efficiently regulate when the patient stands, thus increasing the heart rate. The primary treatment is to strengthen the leg and core muscles to aid in the redistribution of blood.

Since young people, especially those engaged in school sports, are often fitter than adults, the condition is often unknowingly treated by the patient's regular exercise. The condition has become more prevalent since COVID, either from prolonged illness and rest or because athletic activities ceased during quarantine. Young people who had been previously healthy were suddenly lightheaded upon standing and experienced rapid fluctuations in heart rate.

Corlanor is an off-label drug for POTS, and it helps prevent the rapid heart rate. LeAnn couldn't go to physical therapy or engage in intense workouts, so the drug was a good option. Now LeAnn could get up without her heart racing or experiencing shortness of breath.

So, with a new chest port, her POTS under control, the TPN running regularly, LeAnn emerged from a dark tunnel. She was once again able to drive, visit friends, go to lunch, and take trips to visit her children. Life felt stable and manageable once more.

Jennifer's Take:

In September, I was in England visiting my mom. I sent LeAnn a text, and she didn't respond. At first, I thought nothing of it, but that nagging fear wouldn't leave me alone. I tried again and started praying. Something felt wrong;

LeAnn always responded. A few days later, she was able to text me. That's when I discovered she had been in the hospital and gone septic.

"But Don takes it all in stride," she wrote. "He is always patient and kind and rolls with it."

And now our book has moved from the past to the present. LeAnn's fight continues.

When we finally got to catch up in person, we faced each other in LeAnn's cozy living room. I had my cup of tea, I'd pushed the recliner button, and my legs were up. I turned sideways, smiling at LeAnn while Lucy, the canine caregiver, observed. I was ready to get fully caught up.

"Yesterday, my stoma was inflamed," LeAnn told me. "It doesn't happen often, but when it does, the burning and irritation are excruciatingly painful. I was crying, and Don gave me a pain med and said, 'Now remember, by tomorrow, you will wake up and be right as rain.' That's what he likes to say: 'Right as rain.'

"And guess what: this morning I woke up, and he called me from work, and he was correct again."

Right as rain.

The words cycled in my head, and the kindness and patience of "Dr. Don" warmed my heart.

But when LeAnn told me about her procedure to add the chest tube, fear flushed through me, and I tried to keep my face neutral. My thoughts jumbled, wondering whether

Dr. Z really saw a spot for the new chest tube now, or he was just saying he did because he knew LeAnn was almost out of options. Would the antibiotics do their job and stave off any future infection? Would this actually be an outpatient event, or would it result in another two-week hospital stay?

Thankfully, before I showed my fear, LeAnn's phone rang; It was her family checking up on her again. I listened to her half of the conversation, my heart swelling with the love evidenced before me.

Everything about LeAnn's story is unique: her five cancer episodes, her years of living around it and through it, and her brave response to multiple setbacks and bad news. She has remained stalwart and patient and an encourager despite everything. Her hope in Christ buoys her views and outlook. She counters the inevitable negativity and sadness by focusing on others. Right now, she is focusing on her family, and the joy before me dismisses my own fear.

CHAPTER 14

Hope Endures

PRESENT TIME

L eAnn had that new line placed, and just as Dr. Z had said, and Don had predicted, everything went "right as rain." Nine months passed, and LeAnn continued in a stable pattern. Suddenly, she was able to go and do again. The new port, lack of blood clots, POTS management, thyroid medication, and extra hydration was working. She was able to drive, meet friends, and take trips to see her children. She even managed a pool day with me and friends. Granted, she couldn't swim, but often now, "pool day" is simply code for sitting next to a pool and chatting—no swimming required! When I asked her about this newfound stability, her response was profound: "I don't think we can credit any one thing, except that the Lord has laid his hand on my body in a way I cannot describe."

As LeAnn caught up with the ladies, I sat back and listened, wearing what was probably a silly grin. It was beautiful listening to them chat, seeing LeAnn outdoors, enjoying a bit of sun; the only evidence of what she had been through was a line snaking from her bathing suit to her backpack. The scene filled me with joy. It was wonderful to see that bright look of joy in her eyes, which said once again, "Look at me living my best life despite it all."

We sat near the Intracoastal, and again I wished a manatee would swim by, but then I realized we had everything we needed right there: our friend enjoying a beautiful South Florida spring day.

Since her 2020 ostomy surgery, nine months is the longest time LeAnn has ever gone without a hospital stay. But then, a while after our beautiful pool day, LeAnn was back in the hospital with an infected line—but she rallied quickly. There were no visible clots, and the doctors put her on IV antibiotics, switched her line to the other side of the chest, and not long after, released her. According to LeAnn, this was the easiest hospital-stay/line-switch she had ever had. When we spoke, she was upbeat and thankful to be on "her floor" at Good Samaritan Hospital, surrounded by "her people" and getting great care.

After I learned about LeAnn's latest hospital stay, my mind was whirling. The nine-month hiatus before the hospital stay would have been the perfect time to stop the book, because it felt like success. And any time we read a book like this, we want to end it on a successful note. Because this is what we expect from a health saga story:

1. A story of hardship and overcoming.
2. A resolution when the hardship is over, and the overcomer now lives in a beach mansion and skydives from the cliffs at sunrise every morning.

Well, we delivered with number one, but not number two. To be fair, that resolution would be extreme. But isn't that what we all want? We want the hardship behind us, wrapped up in a neat little package, set on the shelf so we can point to it and say, "Wow, look at what they came through, and look what they've achieved."

But real life isn't a movie or a fairy tale. Real life is, well, real life.

Usually, the hardship is there every day with no promise of leaving us. The daily grind of never getting a break can beat us down and make us wonder when enough will be enough. Where is the hope in that?

Most people live with daily hardship. You may live with arthritis or autism or alcoholism or anxiety. And those are just the ones that begin with "a!"

So, what is a person to do? How do we move forward without our resolution, our movie ending where the music is playing as we paraglide off our mountain?

That's when we realize *hope endures*. The best is yet to come, but in the meantime, while we are in the trenches of this difficulty, living it day after day after day, we find our hope in God. Hebrews 6:19 promises us: "Which hope we have as an anchor of the soul, both sure and steadfast."

We have the hope of heaven. But what are we to do in the meantime, in the middle of the day-to-day distress?

We can pray. Prayer doesn't have to be for the big events only. Prayer can be for anything, because God cares about our day-to-day life. Case in point:

Only a few weeks ago, we were re-piping our house. The two-day job had taken over two weeks, and living on and off without running water and with holes in our walls was irritating me. Despite my need for a shower, I was also worried about my dry garden. I know, it's silly in retrospect.

Anyway, clouds had been building all afternoon, and I started praying it would rain on my yard. The clouds were literally right there, dark gray and ominous, promising buckets of rain. But they weren't complying, just threatening. So, I kept praying. Finally, frustrated and immaturely, I decided God must not care about my garden, and I stopped praying about it. It's childish and embarrassing in hindsight.

Five minutes later, my neighbor pulled into the driveway with sheets of drywall in the back of his truck. He hopped out, calling to me to open the garage door, "Oh Jen," he yelled, "I was so scared it was going to rain and ruin all this drywall. I was praying so hard the whole drive. Look at the sky!"

Oh.

My.

Goodness.

How many other times has God withheld answering my prayer with a yes because there was a bigger reason to say no?

I know that's a relatively silly event, but it illustrates a major concept: God hears our prayers, sees our needs, and knows what is best for us. So, my friend, I hope this book helps us all realize that no matter what, we can rest in the fact God sees, knows, and understands everything you are going through.

In conclusion, I want to get personal, dear reader: Do you know God? Is he your Father? Do you know John 3:16 is personally written for you?

"For God so loved the world" means God loves you. "That He gave his only begotten Son" indicates Jesus, who died on the cross for our wrongs. "That whosoever believeth in Him should not perish" shows us putting our faith in Jesus means instead of an eternity separated from God, we shall "have everlasting life"—an eternity in heaven with God. In heaven, there will be no sickness, pain, or suffering but unspeakable joy!

Eternity with God is promised in so many verses. You may have also heard Romans 6:23, which says "the wages of sin is death." It sounds harsh and horrible that the payment for my sin—any sin—is death, but "the gift of God is eternal life through Jesus Christ our Lord." Jesus offers us a gift, the gift of eternal life; we only have to receive it.

Friend, you don't have to be afraid or sad or uncertain. You can place your faith in Jesus today. He can take away your fear. He can give you peace that no matter what you face on earth, you can be assured of an eternity with Him—a healthy eternity, where if you want to paraglide off a mountain, I'm sure you can! There is no magic prayer or words. It simply takes an acceptance in your heart that you believe

Jesus died for you, He will forgive you, and if you ask Him right now, you can become His child. It's that simple: praying with faith, believing his Word, the Bible, and asking Him to save you.

He will!

You will feel the difference immediately. There is no more profound peace or satisfaction than becoming God's child.

So today, may you experience God's hope. May you feel His love, which is freely available to you. In the middle of your heartache, struggle, or questions, may you find confidence and security in a God who loves you more than you'll ever comprehend.

As I think about you, dear reader, and about LeAnn's story, I realize I can't wait to hand LeAnn her story and see her face when she holds her own published narrative of *Hope Endures*. I want her to know her pain and suffering have served a purpose beyond what she can imagine. I want her to know her story will reach people in their darkest times and lift them up because we, my friends, can have *enduring hope*. God, who loves us more than we can comprehend, sees and knows our pain and suffering. Eternity with Him makes the pain in our life on earth a mere blip on the radar.

Yes, life continues. LeAnn's story continues; it is not over. Only God knows what's next, but He is still writing our stories. I will be forever grateful that God allowed my story to intersect with LeAnn's and that, through writing this book, he has gifted me a soul-filling friendship.

So, as we close this book, dear reader, our hope and

prayer for you is that you will know God and know He cares about you—no matter your struggle, pain, trials, or disappointments. Because you too can experience an enduring hope!

With much love,
Jennifer and LeAnn

And then what happened?

If you're like me, and you want to know what happens next, feel free to follow my blog at www.beachhousebusiness.com where I will provide periodic updates to LeAnn's story. You can also find me on instagram at @jenniferarrington_author.

Acknowledgments

I usually write fiction, and when my characters face hardship, I happily inject relief. However, writing a biography offers no such respite.

For this reason, I struggled deeply with completing LeAnn's story. I wanted to mitigate the pain to provide more "easy" days. For this reason, the book was rewritten three times, not to change the story but to present the heartbreaking narrative in a different way.

I'm grateful to the incredible people who provided immense support throughout these rewrites. First, Leah Bendele helped with timeline and point of view issues. Then, my trusted first readers—Karen Ledingham, Dona Lowe, and P.D. Janzen—shared their honest thoughts. And then God led me to Jennifer Crosswhite of Tandem Services. Jennifer provided invaluable developmental and copyedits, giving me guidance and confidence for publication. Debbie Guerrant of Atlas Sky Virtual Solutions, my last-before-I-publish reader, came next, whose proofreading catches even the smallest errors. And finally, a heartfelt thanks to my ARC readers who provided thoughtful suggestions.

To LeAnn - I have tears in my eyes as I write this. LeAnn, you lifted me up when I meant to lift you up. I thank God daily for who you are and what you've taught me. Our bond goes beyond the pages of this book, and I am forever changed by your story.

Ultimately, though, I thank our God, who provides everlasting hope.

Also by Jennifer Arrington

Trusting for Tomorrow - A story of love both lost and found and a mother unafraid to fight for her sick child.

The Counting Tree - A timeless love story of two young people connected by one poignant weeping willow.

Coming Soon: Apex Adventures, a children's adventure series!

All books are listed at www.beachhousebusiness.com